WITH THE *Help of God*

Mara DeRose

PublishAmerica
Baltimore

First printing

PublishAmerica has allowed this work to remain exactly as the author intended, verbatim, without editorial input.

ISBN: 978-1-61546-847-8
PUBLISHED BY PUBLISHAMERICA, LLLP
www.publishamerica.com
Baltimore

Printed in the United States of America

Dedication Page

Thank you Lord for allowing me to create
a book of poems in Your Honor.

Without Your guidance in my life—I'd be an unscripted page.

I would also like to thank my husband Bobby,
my children, Robert Jr. and Kristen for allowing me
the time alone so I could craft what GOD has inspired me to do.

There are many others in my life who have stimulated me,
encouraged me, and held me in their daily prayers so that I could
continue and not give up on my dream of getting this book
published. I am deeply grateful.

Thank you to Publish America for giving an unknown
a chance to achieve a fantasy.

Dedicated to My Blessed Mother

Oh Holy Mary Mother of God,
You gave the world your Son,
A heart that's filled with so much love
To unite our world into ONE.

Oh Holy Mary, Mother of God,
Queen of the Rosary
I offer my daily sufferings
Along with your son, on that tree.

Mother most pure and filled with compassion
I pray for the world in disgrace
We disregard your Son's Holy Words
And tried to live a very fast pace.

I pray for Peace as you have asked
For conversion of sinners and peace
Fill my prayer for things for others
May the numbers in prayers increase?

Thank you for all you do by granting
Help for all humanity!
In my own heart, flood my thoughts with prayer
And bring comfort to the assembly.

Take my prayers please to your Son,
Present my case for me?
You are precious in my eyes
Your Son is holding the key.

Preface

Hello Fellow readers, this is to let you know that most of my poems are meant for music. I've tried my best to write down the notes as best as I could for you. I hope you can get a rough idea how the lyricswere meant to be sung. Alas I'm not gifted when it comes to writing them in music form. I can only TRY and give you an idea. Although I took vocal lessons for ten years I could only read the melody lines from my limited knowledge of Music Theory. For any mistakes—I apologize. I learned mostly by listening "playing by ear" as they say, on the ivories of a piano keyboard.

Contents

A Different Place

A different place, a different time, a different way of wasting time
A different world, a different cover, two different hearts, love one another.
A different planet, a different show, sometimes I don't know which way to go
A different frame, a different race, I try so hard to keep up the pace.
A different clock, a different road, may help me carry this heavy load.

A different man, a different wife, one lasting vow made for life.
A different child, a different teacher, one who knows and will always reach her.
A different river a different sea, one who will carry, one who is real
A different page, a different color, one shining star, to uncover
Times flies by, and stands still; I wonder now, if I ever will.

A different house, a different home, so I won't have to live all alone
A different car, a different jet, I am still wondering is this all I get?
A different job and different joy, I wonder is this your favorite toy?
A different year, and different game, I'm here alone, so alone again.
A different chair, a different street, I wonder who will make my life complete.

A Little Tear

A little tear welled up in the corner of my eye
As I watched and I listened and I prayed
Today is a testimonial for those who have died
Never knowing just what happened on that day.

Nine eleven in two thousand and one
We will never forget the devastation
When the jets flew into the buildings gray
And America cried in frustration.

The Fire-fighters, police and volunteers giving aid
To rescue anyone in the downed buildings
So many lost their lives were heroes made
We must never forget the bravery of spirits willing.

Rescuers going up the stairs,
While workers in the building racing round
Those rescuers never gave a thought to themselves
They just helped others back to the ground.

The heartache I feel as I go through this day
While the list of the names are read
I honor each and everyone that has paid
With their life, and their limb to their grave.

WE will never allow this to happen again
We must keep a vigilant eye
Open up our ears for the secrets of the people
And listen for an answer—or we die…

Nine eleven two thousand and one
Will go down in infamy for sure

It will remain in my heart and my mind
As I remember all the souls to my core!

Now more fire-fighters, police and the forgotten ones
That came to the World Trade Centre
They gave of themselves—tormented still
As the powder from the fire zeroed in
Now are ailing inside their own bodies
And we know how they suffer and defend.

Rise up and help any way you can
To repay all they've done for us
We must not let their actions fade
Allowing their deeds turn to dust.

Now in memory of those heroes that have fallen
Demand that this become a Federal holiday
For they've given—for it was their calling.
We are reminded the price that was paid

Now it's up to us to do our part
By volunteering in ways we are able
Remember those who gave up their lives
And those now resting at HIS Table.

Now each of us must do our part
Reach out to those around your town
Be aware of the hardships that you can fix
All you need do is look around.

Written by: Mara DeRose
Sept. 11th, 2008

And Let Love Be Your Guide

Do you know which path you'll travel on
Do you feel the world spinning round
Do you touch the hand without a sound
And let love be your guide?

Do you know what we wish for you
Do you appreciate what we're telling you
Do you desire what we want for you
And let love be your guide?

Do you search for love and share
Do you know that we'll always care,
Do you explore knowing that we're there
And let love be your guide?

Go forth on the road you chose
Where it will lead,—no one knows
Young woman, We can suppose
And let love be your guide?

Do you seek out the solution for
And smell flowers blooming on God's floor
Do you know there's an open door,
And let love be your guide?

Do you trust those who are leading you
Do you complete what is meant to do
Do you hear what God's asking you
And let Love be your guide?

Written by: Mara DeRose
June 1st, 2009

Anything Is Possible

Anything is possible if we all join hands
And any dream is possible if we choose to stand
Anything can be done if we make a change
And link our voices in various range
Unite our people into one big family
And promote new tasks for you and me.
It's not the valley's—it's not the sea
It's not the asphalt under feet
Nor the color of your skin,
White, black, yellow, thick or thin.
It doesn't matter how you speak
It's united hope that reaches it's peak
Or buildings tall, or planes that fly
Moon or sun or mountains high
Treating your neighbor as yourself
It's now sharing part of your wealth
Anything is possible but we need a dream
We must stand tall, promote the "green"
Anyone can do it, everyone should try
Don't let another day go by
Anything is possible, so begin today
Pray for PEACE and LOVE will stay
If you see someone in need
Offer your gift, and you'll succeed
You will feel such "goodness" inside
Anything is possible, offer your pride
Our country 'tis of thee
Anything is possible if we believe.

Written by: Mara DeRose
January 18, 2009

As I Sit Here

As I sit here with tears in my eyes,
I ponder why my heart cries
I assess why things have gone wrong
And I wonder why I'm so all alone.

As I sit here with thoughts in my head
I wonder why I can't sleep in my bed
It isn't a surprise that worries me.
My thoughts are racing and haunting

As I sit here questioning what I think
My self esteem is beginning to shrink
My page is empty, I've run out of ink
I've come to the bitter end am I on the brink?

As I sit here trying to convey
All the happenings of this very day
I marvel each moment that I am alive
How in this world did I survive?

I feel as if I've lost every friend
And that my road is—at last at an end
A Phenomenon has happened to others around
Why is it that I'm here—where am I bound?

Where is that woman I once called me?
Why does my heart ache, why can't I be free
My thoughts keep repeating over again
As I sit here, without being able to mend.

As I sit here starring at the blank walls
It's as if I had never lived, or heard life's calls

As I sit here with my arms open wide
No wonder my heart does cry, cry, cry.

Written by: Mara DeRose
August 16, 2008

Autumn

The first leaf of autumn fluttered down from the tree
First one—then another...they go where they please
The squirrels run the gauntlet of gathering their swill
Scampering up and down as they gather their fill
The breeze becomes cooler dispensing colors round
Foliage from tree stems come airlessly down
And nights linger longer, as the sun fades and sets
More sleepy with milieu,—splendor I can't forget
Streets are more tranquil with children in school
Everyone's knowing—autumn's in rule
It's time that I take—a long, awesome walk
With winter soon calling, and breezes do talk
The crunch and the munch, that quickens my pace
But I keep on moving—from space to place
I notice winds scuffling—dusting the ground
Dispersing it's swirling, as it touches down
Time to put in bed,—bulbs for the spring
Gathering scant flowers—bringing them in
We soon seal all windows, latch all the doors
Cover up the bushes, sweep up the floors
For the first leaf of autumn will soon be the last
And Autumn soon leaves me, gazing through glass

Written by: Mara DeRose
Sept. 17, 2008

AVE Maria (New Version)
Oh Mother pure oh Mother chase oh Mother kind to the human race
oh Mother You're for ever in my heart
Ab
Low G

Ave Maria
(NEW MUSICAL VERSION)

Ave Maria, Ave Maria, Ave Maria
Maria

Ave Maria, Ave Maria, Ave Maria,
Ave Maria…

Oh Mother Pure, Oh Mother Chaste
Oh Mother kind to the human race,
Oh Mother your forever in my heart

Oh Mother kind, Oh Mother Sweet
Oh Mother you make my life complete
Oh Mother, your forever in my heart

Oh Mother dear I ask of you
To turn your eyes and grant us too
Oh Mother you're forever in my heart

Oh Mother now I beg of you
To end all wars and sickness too
Oh Mother your forever in my heart

On Mother's Day I turn to You
I'm asking what you'd have me do
On Mother your forever in my heart

Please pray for me, please pray for me
I'm asking you down on bended knee
Oh Mother you're forever in my heart.

Oh Mother meek, Oh Mother mild
You gave the world your son crucified
Oh Mother, your forever in my heart!

Written by: Mara DeRose
May 4th, 2009

Ave Maria Pre-Hymn

Ave Ma ri a Ave Ma ri a Ave Mari a

low D

Ave Ma ria

Be Careful What You Wish For

Be careful what you wish for,
It may not be what you want
Be careful what your heart says
For it may come back to haunt
So Follow your dreams,
Don't wish your life away,
Happiness is a state of mind
So remember that as you pray.

Be careful what you wish for,
Happy is as happy does,
Grin and bear it ever day
Don't be too quick to judge
Better to be safe than sorry
Keep your friendships in repair
Every picture tells a story
Trust in Him and don't despair

Clouds gather before a storm
It is better to give than receive
Butterflies come to pretty flowers
They flutter amongst the leaves
God gave music to calm our hearts
To fill our souls with peace
So do His work with all your might
And your life will never cease.

Be careful what you wish for
Take heed in what you need
Travel on this road of life
And be careful of your speed

For everyday is a gift from God,
So be careful what you do
Be careful what you wish for
It may be coming true…

Written by: Mara DeRose
Aug. 31, 2009

Birthdays

Sorrows make us human
Failures keep us humble
Success keeps you going
But only GOD keeps you growing.

Happiness keeps you sweet
Tribulations leave you strong
Beauty is but skin deep
Perseverance is my song

Love deeply each day
Care completely along the way
Promise fulfillment as you should
Speak kindly—if you would

Aspire to inspire others
Give it as a lift
Leave Everything to GOD
As Birthdays are a gift.

Written by: Mara DeRose
July 9, 1964

Bits and Pieces

Bits and pieces, of dreams in my life
I'd like a slice not a crumb
I need a" whole" not a fragment—nor strife
Is this too much to over-come?

Everyone has happiness around
Or is it that I just don't see
Am I'm really the one whose the clown?
Where's the girl that use to be me?

Do I expect too much out of life
Where is my piece of the pie?
I have so much "stuff" and much strife
As the years go scurrying by

Why do I feel so alone all the time?
Find the JOY other's have
Why must I search for the rhyme?
Sometimes life is so sad.

If only all my dreams could come true
If only the love is fulfilled
If only all the stresses would just melt away
Why must I be so strong willed?

Right now I'd settle for a smidgeon of peace
A cut, a portion, a chard
God will one day bring His release
I'll find some without being tired?

Fragments, smidgeons and chunks of my days
Am I expecting too much?
Morsels, crumbs and traces of age
I pray that one day I'll be touched!

Bread & Wine, Body and Blood

Body and Blood, Bread and Wine,
Christ you gave us, the world to shine
Light and Dark, sun and moon,
Open my heart, as you opened the tomb.

Come to me, my Lord, My God,
I give you Thanks, I offer my love
I pray today, you'll help me see
Your body and blood has set me free.

Thanks be to Mother Most Chaste
Thanks to St Joseph,, no time to waste
Thanks to the Trinity, especially your Son
Through his sufferings, into His kingdom come.

I am unworthy, I am with stain
I have so much to lose and gain
Wash away my guilt, and grant to me
Your body and blood and set me free.

Thanks be to Mother Most Chaste
Thanks to St Joseph, no time to waste
Thanks to the Trinity, especially your Son
Through his sufferings, into His kingdom come.

Butterfly

Butterfly with your wings of orange, black and gold
How long does it take to let your pretty wings unfold?
Butterfly, you're here and there and then you fly away
Butterfly I hope that you'll be back again one day.

Butterfly, you flit between the blossoms of each flower
Butterfly, the sunlight's bright and still you hover by the hour
Butterfly, do you have a home and do you have a love so rare
Butterfly, I long to be just like you, while floating on the air.

Butterfly, you flit between the flowers by the hour
Butterfly, spread your wings gathering nectar from each flower
Butterfly you float on the breeze and never question anyone
Butterfly, I'd like to fly with you, until my work is done.

Butterfly, how I wished that I could fly
Butterfly, spread my wings and travel high up in the sky
Butterfly, I'd create the best poem that I could write
Then, disappear and soar into HIS Heavenly sight.

Written by: Mara DeRose
January 14, 2009

Cadence

The cadence pulsates through the air
I wonder why, I wonder where
It's beat keeping echoing in my ear
I live my life without a care.

The rhythm of the ocean's roar
It's out to sea, dancing cross it's floor.
The birds soar high braving their plight
Diving for food, back up to the light.

Whipping of the howling trees
Amidst the rumbling on the breeze
Quivering through the knurly knoll
Up and down, takes it's toll.

Rain as it's puddles on the ground
Drip, drip drop, it's motion found
It cascades into a rivulet flow
It answers to no one, it searches below.

Comets streaking across the sky
'Nary a sound, on it's fly
It greats the planets one by one
Before it implodes, after it's run.

Children playing on the merry go round
Laughing in ecstasy, as it rotates around
And deep inside, they have no fears
They live their lives, with plenty of tears.

The cadence spawns a song in fall
It is embellished with awesome call
And scampers down through my brain
It answers to God—and will remain.

Written by: Mara DeRose
September 7, 2008

Candy Cane Lane

Santa's coming down Candy Cane Lane
He's humming to himself, it's Christmas time again
My reindeer fly into the night
Making all that's merry, and all that's bright.
Candy Cane Lane is next on my list
I wonder if Johnny will share his gift?
I'll climb upon the roof tops tall
And press my finger till I am small
That chimney is sure to give me trouble
I'll blink my eye and go down on the double.
Fill up each stocking for the good boys and girls
Then eat all the cookies and away I'll whirl
Onto the next house on Candy Cane Lane
I wonder if Eric would like a train
A dolly for Susie, and a game or two
Then press my finger and I'll go up the flue
Oh my goodness I dropped my hat
This jolly old guy is old and fat.

2001 Cells of Destruction

Cells of destruction, in our land,
Deceiving those with their devious plan.
The hijackers flew into the building's gray
Bringing disaster along the way.
Innocent people aboard those flights
WE remember their spirits in honored light.
We thought our world was safe and secure,
We mourn for those that live no more.
Into the towers of World Trade Center
The smoke that billowed from every angle
The towers started to slowly crumble
Killing so many and amidst the tangle
Ashes, steel intertwined, and mangled
Glued to the TV and watched the horror
I feel so helpless, where is tomorrow?
Just as we thought they were safe in their toil
Down came another building, into the soil.
Working around the clock day and night
Will there ever be an end to this plight?
May God Bless those who gave their lives?
Never knowing how America cries.
Let us be a catalyst to affirm
By helping others, let our candles burn.
Caregivers, with your hands and feet
Let God allow your talents to greet
Find those who may be still alive
Guide their efforts, help them survive
Shattered dreams we rebuild, renew
We the people who put their trust in You.
Unite us all with Unity
Let our fabric show to all humanity.

Written by: Mara DeRose
September 11, 2001

Christ In Christmas

For on such a heavenly night
Christ was born in a hallowed light.
May we sleep in heavenly peace
And may He Bless us—as we sleep
Mary and Joseph searching a place
Angels choirs sing to HIS crowning face
Peace on earth and mercy mild
Welcome HIM—this heavenly child.
The ox and ass, shepherds and kings
Come adore this child Mary brings
The first Noel, the story told
The star shone bright along the road.

Guide us to this heavenly sight
All is silent, In the still of night.
So this is Christmas—What child is this
Another year over, a Savior kiss.
Hark the Harold, Glory to the new born king
Ave Maria, Bless her name unto her a baby came
OH holy Night, the stars are brightly shining
Do you hear what I hear, in heaven above
Ringing out cloud and clear
Oh Little Town of Bethlehem
Away in a manger, no crib for a bed
May He find sweet shelter for HIS Sweet head.

Written by: Mara DeRose
Dec. 5th, 2008

My Christmas Poem '04

My Christmas candle is lit with Blessings from above
For Christmas candles symbolizes light, hope and love
My Christmas candles placed around my house and tree
Reminding me just how precious life can be.

I kneel and pray as I see the candles burn
I pray for Peace, Faith so Jesus will return.
Mother Mary be with us day and into the night
And always guide my steps towards His heavenly light.

Family gather around, and my spirit seems to sing
As we move closer around the piano, my heart begins to sing
All the classic Carols as the candles flicker with cheer
As I recite a silent prayer to GOD, that only He can hear.

My Christmas gift to my friends and family
It is free for the taking, just ask HIM and you'll see
Follow His rules and go where He leads
Turn to HIM, trust in HIM and you will succeed.

My Christmas candle gently glows with His divine light
For it's because of His birth, that He arrive on Christmas night
So when you search for guidance, look no further than your heart
For God is truly in You—as long as you do your part.

Christmas 2008 A Special Song

I don't know how reindeer fly
And I don't know how Santa gets so high
And Charlie Brown and his Christmas tree
Brings us cheer on Christmas eve
Every time a bell does ring
And Angel gets it's heavenly wings
The Grinch soon learns from all the "Who"
Down in Whoville—with Tiny Lou
White Christmas is sung again in dreams
While Sugar-plum fairies dance the theme
Rudolph with his nose so red
While children nestled in their beds
Stockings hung by the chimney with care
Oh Christmas tree is standing there
Holiday Inn brings holiday songs
Little Drummer Boy, his gift so strong
Jingle Bells ring all the way
In a one horse open sleigh
In the stillness of the sight
WE all can sing our Silent Night
The chipmunks singing in the tree
There's some "roast beast" for you and me.
Christmas, Christmas time for JOY
I just want a hoola hoop…Oh Boy!
Let it snow, let it snow as the year ends
Should old acquaintance always friend

For on such a heavenly night
Christ was born in a hallowed light.
May we sleep in heavenly peace
And may He Bless us—wars to cease
Mary and Joseph searching a place

Angels choirs sing to HIS crowning face
Peace on earth and mercy mild
Welcome HIM—this heavenly child.
The ox and ass, shepherds and kings
Come adore this child Mary brings
The first Noel, the story told
The star shone bring, along the road
Guide us to this heavenly sight
All is silent, I the still of night.
So this is Christmas
Another year over, a new one of cheer

Written by: Mara DeRose
Dec. 5th, 2008

Christmas In My Heart

Everyday is Christmas if you just let it be
The happiness of every minute is there for all to see
For Jesus Christ is born today in my heart and mind
For he gave up his life for us, and that of all mankind.

Our Lady gave birth to Jesus with the Angels all around
And in the east the star shone down and Joseph stood on Holy Ground
The wise men came and brought him gifts, of gold and frankincense and myrrh
It was foretold that He would come, and bring the world a stir…

I live my life accordingly, because of that blessed day
I will honor and worship HIM especially when I pray.
Christmas comes but once a year
And we celebrate HIS birth
Let us never forget his tender heart
Let us praise him for all we're worth.

Christmas Is a Coming

Christmas is a coming
Spread it all around
You see it on the streets
All around the town
Holiday lights are blinking
Red, green and white
Snow flakes are falling
Oh what a beautiful sight
Christmas is a coming
You hear it everywhere
Carols sung on the corner
In the middle of the square.
Santa's getting ready
For his yearly ride
Gifts for all good children
Oh what a surprise.
Christmas is a coming
Stockings hung up to receive
All those little trinkets
That Santa Claus may leave
I wish you Merry Christmas
And a Blessed New Year
I hope you have good fortune
For happiness and cheer.

Christmas Poem

Snow flurries are predicted
Shopper rushing, spirits lifted
Light are blinking, holly's twisted
Carolers strolling, snow has shifted

Presents wrapped under the tree
Santa's taking another peek
Fire is crackling, could that be?
Holiday music surrounds me?

Christ is born in Bethlehem
Renew our spirits, throughout the land
Grant us blessings and your plan
Take and lead us by YOUR HAND?

All is silent, all is still
Hearts are happy, and are filled
Children sledding down the hill
Families gather, feel the chill?

Sons and daughters, nary a groan
Safe and warm by the phone
Now I won't be all alone
All is happy in our home.

Christmas 2007

Another year has come and gone
Another reason that's come along
Another reason to gather around
Friends and family we count upon.

Ring out the old and bring in the new
Trust in yourself—and others too
Embrace each day with tender care
Remember those who are not there.

Spiritual and emotional nourishment
Give to your heart in accomplishment
We never know—for the road is bent
To take it all in, and life you've spent.

Turn to family here before
Gather them in, with love galore
Never let it be said, your heart is alone
For God has granted this year past flown

Merry Christmas, Happy New Year family and friends
Know that your friendship has been wisely spent
Rest assured YOU are prayed for each day
As the old year slowly passes away.

Chards

There are chards of crystals in the night sky above
When hearts are deep in passion and in love
Refracted prisms deep within your eyes
And the heart is filled with satisfaction and tries
And love prevails upon those who are unsuspecting
And the mind and body quiver with anticipation.

Chards of diamonds—sparklettes in the snow
And the crisp winter air is on the flow
Open up those feelings of happiness within
And greets the mind and the body again.
Attacks the senses and with delight
Brings you warmth—on a cold winter's night.

Collage of Colors

I see a collage of colors
Splashing waves upon the beach
The moments when we touched
Everything was in our reach

Ripples in a brook
When a stone is skipped across
See the "sparklettes" of the sunlight
Come radiating, then are lost

Music, wine and candles
Reminds me of wonderful times
Melodies linger longer
They just play on in my mind.

I give to you a flower
You give to me a ring
We all live happily ever after,
Life is a wonderful thing.

Snow that flies in winter
There's a harshness everywhere
Aroma of some flowers,
Will liven up the air…

Taste and seek the truth
Looking high and low
When you do discover
You'll find happiness in tow?

Colors of My Life

Rainbow coating on the sun-kissed sky above
Make one stop and think of love
Raging waters gushing towards the sea
Kites fly high above the tree.

Flower peeking through the dampened earth
Raising it's head, sharing it's worth
Trees quiver in the sustaining air
They seem not to have a care

Roads that bend and wind along
But we never hear its throng—
As we watch a blade of grass grow
I wonder about the winter snow…

Journey through time, day by day
Thrusting its gears to take me away
Ripples of raindrops as they fall
Watch all humans as they learn to crawl…

Fragrant aromas scenting the air
Birds in flight; watch if you dare
Lips that pass truth refreshes my silence
Are all shining examples of life in compliance?

Written By: Mara DeRose
May 17, 20001

Come On In

Come on in and sit right down
Take a seat and we'll chat
I It's been so long since you've been here
Don't worry about your hat.

Come on in and visit with me
I've missed your smiling face
It's been so long since you've been gone
Don't worry about my place.

Come on in and stay awhile
I'll make you a cup of tea
I'm so very happy to see you
I'll give you a spare key.

Come on in and rest awhile
You look tired from your ride
I know how hungry you must be
Won't you like a piece of humble pie?

Come on in and join me now
We'll stroll down memory lane
We'll not bother with "formalities"
Come on in out of the rain.

Come on in and we'll discuss
Anything that's on your mind
I'm here for you my friend
We've stood the test of time.

Come on in and be my guest
I'll prepare a room for you
I hope you'll stay for a visit
Because my heart has truly missed you.

Come Play With Me

Come play with me, and walk right in
Come dance along my beach
The rhythms of it's watery sprays
My heart beneath it's reach.

Come walk, come prance upon my shore
And perceive the ocean's song
The cadence of your heart beat
Will assist you stroll along.

The birds foraging for each meal
Diving further onto the floor
Cawing to one another
Along the ocean's door.

Come play with me, and walk right in
Come hobble amid the stones
Come stepping over the seaweed
While shuffling through it's foam.

Stride right in, and jump the waves
Come play with me if you will
For I am always with you
My beauty, and my chill.

Ride upon my back and surf
My breakers are in command
Memories will linger longer
When you saunter upon my sand.

So come on in, and stay awhile
And enjoy it while you can
I am here waiting for you
Come often when I expand.

Dearest Grandmother

Dearest Grandmother, I am singing you this song
To tell you all the feelings that I feel.
Dearest Grandmother, while I'm singing you your song
I hope you'll want to sing along
And know how much I truly care.

When I looked into your big blue eyes
I can see all the years of wisdom hidden there
I can see all the happiness and caring there
I feel Your love…

When I look upon your aging face
Glowing with that style and giving grace
Always striving to keep up the pace
I feel your warmth.

You look like a butterfly, spreading her wings
As if you could get up and fly
With dignity and beauty as you pass by
It's no wonder why you are loved…

So dearest Grandmother, as we celebrate your day
I h9ope these memories won't fade away
May God bless you forever and a day
Because honestly you are loved…

Written by: Mara DeRose
  July 14, 1981 Grandma's birthday!
  Died July 31st, 1990

Did You Know

Did you know that I was the one who stood beside you day and night
And did you know that I was the one who tried to show you how to make very thing alright
For all times, I've been there when you came with questions needing answers not revealed
And I will be there when you need some answers yes, indeed.

Did you know that I'm the one who took your side when troubles came and went
And did you know that I'm the one who also sat with you and come to your defense
Did you know that no matter what you've said to me, I've forgiven you my son
That one day soon, you'll come on home and we'll begin all over again.

Did you know that years have come and gone without your seeing
That my heart was inside out and always so concerning
I'd give you up and start anew if You'd give me one more chance
Did you know, you're my son and I need to have

Did you know that as a child you were so close to me
And did you know that as you grew I chose to set you free
I tried my best to show you how to become a man
Now my son, in your heart of heart be strong and face each day you've planned.

Did you know that no matter which way you decide to go
That I'll be here, waiting just for you, to help put on your show
I've learned my lesson, and I'll never make that mistake again
I hope you know, that I'm trying my best to slowly make amends.

Do You Believe

Do you believe in the birth of Christ
In Bethlehem 2000 so years ago
The angel that appeared that night
And the stars that were all aglow

Mary and Joseph traveled along
To pay their taxes due
As Mary's time grew near
Joseph searched for shelter—few

Do you believe in the gift of faith
And do you believe in love
Do you believe in Jesus Christ
And His truth and strength from above?

Do you celebrate this holiday
Just with trinkets and with things
Do you push away all your fears and cares
And allow Christmas to come in?

Do you prepare for the Holy event
Offering HIM all you can give
Remembering that Our Savior was sent
Shout with joy and forgive.

Do you celebrate His Holiday
Prepare your soul from sin
So give to others in need as you pray
And allow Christmas to enter in.

Does Anyone Really Know Me?

Does anyone really know me?
Does anyone really care?
Does anyone ever think of me
Whenever they come there?

Does anything ever matter?
Do people see me as I see?
Does anyone know the meaning
Or is it a game of hide and seek?

Do I pretend to know all the answers?
To questions that that my heart wants to know
And does my family respect me?
Or do they do that just for a show?

I have so many questions,
I will tell you what's inside
If you want to know me better
Scratch the surface of my pride

Does anyone really KNOW me?
Can you tell me if you do
Because the woman I see there
Has nothing but an excuse.

Does anyone take a moment?
To seek out what maybe
The heart—of one woman
And that woman is only ME.

Does anyone really know me?
Does anyone pursue the clues?
Does anyone take the time
I hope that one day, they do…

Does anyone ever ask me?
How I feel about my life
And do they stop for an answer
For the answer is my light.

Do You Take

Do you take this woman—to be your lawfully wedded wife
Do your promise to protect her,—Will you love her all your life?
Will you be honest and trust her—and promise to be true
Will you tell her everyday—that her heart belongs to you?
Place a ring upon her finger, and she in turn gives one to you
Seal your love forever with something borrowed, something blue.
The Unity candle is glowing and as the music begins to peel
You turn and face each other, sharing exactly how you feel.
Receding down the aisle hand in hand, man and wife
You travel on together, making memories all your life
With each day that lay before you, and each night a chance to learn
You will walk each road in toil, offering your concern.
There will be days of sorrow, and there will be days of bliss
There will be many a heartache, you can answer with a kiss.
In those days of great pleasure, know there will be a little rain
And with the help of God, he'll ease you through the pain.
From this moment on, you will now be as one flesh
You will live and love with all your might, and we wish you happiness
One thing will never change now, one thing that will come true
You go with all God's Blessing and His light's shining down on you.
If you should have some children, if you should leave the town
If you should go into a room, and feel it falling round
Remember to look back now, remember this very day
Your heart will cry in happiness, and your tears will melt away.
You are now man and wife and let no one break apart
For you have one another and a whole new start
So smile at one another, and remember as you seek
That all of us around are happy for your life is now complete.

Written by: Mara DeRose
July 24, 2008

Dulcet Voice I Hear

It's your dulcet voice I hear in the night
Crying out from the beyond,
God has whisked you away from my sight
Melodious tune echoes our bond.

How I miss the soothing sound your voice made
Its melody repeats in my brain
I long to envelope my thoughts as I wait
On life's journey—a clickety-clack train.

Now as I wait to join you my dear
God has other plans for me now
I listen for your voice through my tears
And wished I could see your smile.

It's your sweet voice that lingers each day
And memories flood into dreams at night
I'm lonely for a heavenly bouquet
These vespers keep impinging my flight.

I—now, alone in my room
Staring at these Spartan walls
Trickling around the sounds in my tomb
I have no place till I fall.

Written by: Mara DeRose
October 14, 2008

During My Novena

During my Novena today
I heard my Mother say
That she was in a better place
And at peace in every way.

Auntie has come to join her
And that someday her sisters will join
And they can all be happier
Since the day that they were born.

Jesus will smile upon them
And allow them to see one another
And Grandma will come to greet each
As she did for each of your brothers.

As I say my prayers to God
And ask for his divine Mercy
I know you'll one day be near by
To greet me, and to kiss me.

I thank you now again Father
For giving me this time with her
I thank you for all the kindness
And I know I always will.

Written by: Mara DeRose
March 3, 2005

It's true that I heard MOM's voice and then saw her face during the 4th decade of the Rosary. She told me Aunt Marion was with her, and I heard Aunt Marion say YEAH…the way she always spoke when she was alive. Mom told me that she forgave me my trespasses.

Easter Eggs and Bunny

It's that special time of year
When the Easter Bunny comes
He brings those Easter eggs
And he runs, and runs and runs.

While you are asleep
He jumps into your home
He Fills your Easter Basket
While he is there alone.

Eggs decorated in many hues
Jelly beans galore
He hides the chocolate bunnies
In plants, or some in drawers.

He brings you little gifts
In colors for the spring
He hops and hops around
And in his heart he sings

Easter eggs and jelly beans
Blue, pink and green
Bunnies and chicks in chocolate
The cutest you've ever seen

Blue and black and lavender
Yellow, white and red
I wonder which one of you
Will lop off the bunny's head?

So while you eat your tasty treats
Remember Easter Bunny
He'll be coming round
Cause it's a treat for your tummy.

When you wake to Easter morn
You take the time to pray
And thank the Lord above
For the Love He's given today.

You are my greatest Easter treat
I lay my burdens at your feet
Because I am so very weak
And I know you are so meek

I will not answer to defeat
Because I know you are so sweet!
You died for me upon the cross
And from the start you've been the boss

All my inhibitions toss
And I'm at a word of loss
For you walked upon the earth
Always knowing since my birth.

Fine Line

I'll be walking a fine line
I'll be tasting a fine wine
I'll be having a fine time
As long as you're with me

I'll be walking a fine line
I'll be making a high climb
Cause I want to know you're mine
As long as you're with me.

I don't want you to ever doubt my love
I need you besides me everyday.
And if I ever make you doubt my love
I hope and pray—you'll want me to stay.

So I'll be walking a fine line
I won't be straying cause you're mine
Toast our love with this fine red wine…
As long as you're with me.

I've learned my lesson and now I see
That your heart belongs for only me
You opened up the door and here's the key
Cause today your gonna marry me.

Yes, I am walking a fine line
Soon we'll hear those wedding chimes
I'll love you even more that I did before
Have no doubts…I'm yours forever more.

Written by: Mara DeRose
August 2, 2008

First Anniversary in Heaven

Close your eyes and go to sleep
Close your eyes and don't you peek
Sandman's coming soon my dear,
Hush now dearest Mama.

God has taken you by HIS HAND
You are in his Heavenly land
Rest assured I'm taking care
While you sleep my Mama.

I remember your words to me
Help my sibling and I will see
Give to Papa your strength each day
Always remember me when you pray.

Close your eyes and go to sleep
Close your eyes and don't you peek,
Sandman has come and gone you see
Sprinkled your "Dust" all over me.

No more suffering, no more pain
No more standing out in the rain
No more worrying, they're all gone you see.
Now you can rest for ETERNITY.

Fooling Myself

Each day I live is just like the last
I don't know why, I just cling to the past
This is the question, I longing to know
Why is it difficult to just let you go?

Fooling myself is the thing I do best
There goes my dreams and you know the rest
Should I have left you a long time ago
But in my heart, I'm still loving you so.

I thought that you were the perfect lover
How I was fooled and soon would discover
You took my heart, my soul and my mind
All I have left is heartaches and time.

Truly I loved you, and I don't know why
I guess this is best, and that is no lie
Don't bother to phone, just allow me to cry
How could you ever tell me "goodbye?"

Each day that I live is just like the last
I don't know why I cling to the past
I hope someone will answer my plea
So leave me alone and just let me be!

*Ever in My Heart****

Jesus Christ, I praise your Holy Name,
Lord above, all the earth kneels before you
Come and take, away—all the pain
Ever in my heart—You remain.

Lamb of God I seek your Holy Door
Ever In my payer. . . You're the one I adore
Come to me and teach me how to live
Ever in my soul
Ever in my soul
Ever in my soul. You shall live!

Words of Christ stay with me night and day,
Praises sing on my lips—this I do pray
Heal my mind and that of all mankind,
Ever in my heart,
Ever in my voice,
Ever in my soul—each day!

Forgive Me, I'm Sorry

Each time I look at you, I just wanna say
I'm sorry, forgive me
For leaving you alone that way.

Each time I see you, and you see my face
I'm sorry, forgive me
I didn't mean to hurt you it's my disgrace

Each time I looked into your big brown eyes,
I'm sorry, forgive me
I didn't mean to tell you lies.

Each time I've walked away and left you alone
I'm sorry, forgive me
Please allow me to phone.

Cause you know that I love you,
and I didn't mean to hurt you
But in saying that I'm sorry,
and I'm hoping that I can make it up somehow.

Each time I looked at you from day one,
I knew you were the only one
Please love me, and forgive me
I'll never do that again…

Each time I've hurt you by my deceit
I'll make it up to you, and be discreet
I'll pay the price whatever you want
Just forgive me cause it's all I want.

Cause you know that I love you,
And I didn't mean to hurt you
But by saying that I'm sorry dear,
I hope you'll forgive me and allow me near…

Written by: Mara DeRose
January 24, 2008

God and Me

Love is a powerful confirmation
Of emotions and salutations
Affirming breaths, I must inhale
Recharging my battery, or I will fail.

Renewal that I have been created to express
Healing touches of HIS handiness.
Peace-filled hearts fortify our minds
Unity of spirit, for all mankind.

Considerate, nonjudgmental and accepting of truth
Whirlpool of activities, bouquets the vermouth,
Tranquility of spirit exuding from within
Experience from my willingness to win.

Anchor me for I need Your control
Bring forth a rainbow, spirit my soul
I've become aware of unlimited possibilities
That s why I'll THANK YOU, down on my bended knees.

Happy Birthday in Heaven

Happy Birthday in HEAVEN, My Love
It's been many years since
I heard your voice,
gazed into your eyes,
touched your hand,
kissed your lips, held you near.
My heart is broken, my soul is lost,
my life is empty.
Everyday I miss you.
The pain does not go away.
I had been waiting for you
my entire life.
To share a love too special
words cannot convey.
We loved each other so deeply,
so fully with our hearts,
minds, bodies and spirits.
Our time together was too short
but the love we shared,
the love I will always have for you,
will fill me my entire lifetime.
I will be forever thankful and
grateful for every moment
spent with you.
I was not your first love,
but I am and was your last love.
Hugs as always

Have I Told You

Have I told you how much I love you?
Have I shared with you my thanks too
Have I presented you today, my gratitude and say
That you are my hero, as well as my Aunt.

Have I told you how much I care
And how many times I wished I were there
I would offer you a hug, and never have a shrug
That you are my hero, and my friend.

Have I told you how special you are
And I'm glad that God has given me your star
Have I offered you a sign, and brought you my mind
That you are my hero, and my bud(dy).

Have I told you how much you've encouraged me
Every day something happens allowing me
If I change my attitude, and I will soon exude
Cause you're my hero, and I can always trust in YOU.

Have I mentioned how helpful you have been
I'm always treated special and it seems
That no matter what I do, you always see me through
Cause you're my hero, you my friend, and I love Y OU…

His Garden

Through the gates of Heaven into HIS Garden
The flowers and trees are ever growing
The rives and streams are cascading in rhythm
I picture it now, and gladly go with HIM.

I see my Great Grandma, and there's Uncle John
And then I se Mother Mary, and HI Father Tom
I'm so ecstatic at these delights
I give all my thanks to these sacred sights.

Music I hear fills my soul with much peace
It over-flows into such sweet release
My Lord and my God is waiting to hear
All the souls of the world, He's accepting this year.

I go to my Mother and kiss her hello
I ell her how I've missed her and still love her so
God's love enfolds you my daughter this day
He's allowed you to enter His Garden to pray!

My expectations were nothing like this
The garden ageless and timeless created in wish
My soul is so peaceful I linger and pray
"Oh God, allow me into your garden to stay?"

Hi Grandpa, Aunt Helen, Father Lane
HI Moses, Mother Theresa and HI to all of my friends
Thank you LORD, thank you Father, this I do pray
For inviting me into YOUR GARDEN today

I Am An Ordinary Woman

I am an ordinary woman
And Yes, my eyes are blue
I live and love and laugh and cry
Just like most women do.

I have some thoughts inspired
With hopes and dreams for you
I want and need, and give and please
Just like I ought to do.

I am an ordinary Mother
And yes, I even bend
I try and cry, and hope to try
Just like a long lost friend.

I am an ordinary sister
And yes, I care too much
I want the best, and second guess
Just to keep us fresh.

I am an ordinary lady
But I go that extra mile
I cook and clean, and in between
I take the time to sigh.

I am an ordinary woman
And yes, I've learned to love
I work and play, but everyday
I never forget to pray.

And in my ordinary day
I include you in my life

I try and say, with words in play
Just like I want to do…

Yes, I'm an ordinary woman
And I've loved my life thus far
I'll clean and sew, and never let go
Cause that's what I'm to do…

And when my time runs out
And God takes me back home
I'll sing and dance, and shout and prance
All Glory is to you…

Written by: Mara DeRose
March 17, 2009

I Believe in Christmas

I Believe In Christmas

Oh, I believe in Christmas—just as I believe in love
Yes, I believe in Christmas—just as sure as they are a trillion stars above.
And I believe in Miracles and I believe in YOU
And I believe in Angels, for I found an angel in YOU.
Everyday I hold in my heart a wish—for Christmas to be in each one's heart
Every night I dream of Peace and Hope, and the cures that will come from heaven above.
And I'll hold on to that dream of mine, until the day will come
When Jesus fills me up Grace and gives—the world it's daily dose of love.
Oh Oh, I believe,—Oh, I believe, Oh, I believe in Christmas
Oh, I believe,—oh I believe oh, I believe in Love
Oh, I believe, Oh, I believe—Oh, I believe where there are miracles
Wishing you a Christmas filled with God's love.

Oh, I believe in Christmas,—just as sure as I know my own heart
Yes, and I believe in family, and the message of peace and love to start.
And I believe and trust in HIM, when even on my worst day
And I believe in Christmas and I will until God comes to take it all away.
So Please go out and celebrate the good news, for Jesus is asking us to do
And fill your heart with the gifts he gives, each day to you and you and you…
For I believe in in Christmas, just as I believe in YOU
And I believe in OUR LORD above without Him what would this entire world do?

Oh, I believe in Holiness and asking for one's needs
And I believe in Prayer and Peace, just as I know He's helping me succeed
And I believe in Miracles, and I believe in YOU
And I believe in Angels, for you're my angel…you're my Christmas
God Bless YOU.

Oh Oh, I believe,—Oh, I believe, Oh, I believe in Christmas
Oh, I believe,—oh I believe oh, I believe in Love

Oh, I believe, Oh, I believe—Oh, I believe where there are miracles
Wishing you a Christmas filled with God's love.

Written by: Mara DeRose
November 2008

This is my Christmas Song I've just finished writing and I wished I could have put it down so you could hear it. Again, unfinished plans but dreams of how it would be someday.

God Bless you, and bring us Peace, Joy and Happiness now and always.
Merry Christmas and Happy Blessed New Year 2009

I Don't Know Why

I don't know how reindeer fly
They whisk Santa off into the sky
And Charlie Brown and his Christmas tree
Brings us cheer on Christmas Eve
Every time a bell does ring
And Angel gets it's heavenly wings
The Grinch soon learns from all the "Who"
Down in Whoville—with Betty Lou
White Christmas is sung again in dreams
While Sugar-plum fairies dance the theme
Rudolph with his nose so red
While children nestled in their beds
Stockings hung by the chimney with care
Oh Christmas tree is standing there
Holiday Inn brings holiday songs
Little Drummer Boy, his gift so strong
Jingle Bells ringing all the way
In a one horse open sleigh
In the stillness at the Holy sight
WE all can sing our Silent Night
The chipmunks singing in the tree
There's some "roast beast" for you and me.
Christmas, Christmas time for JOY
I want a hoola hoop…Oh Boy!
Let it snow, let it snow as the year ends
Should old acquaintance always friend
It's the most wonderful time of the year
So I'll be home for some Holiday Cheer
Santa's stepping down candy cane lane
As we'll be rocking around and saying again
Have Yourself a Merry Little Christmas
And Auld Lang Syne, don't be kissed- less

Under the Mistletoe and Holly
Put away for another years folly
Now I wish you a Happy New Year
One with Heath, and so much cheer.

Written by: Mara DeRose
Dec. 5th, 2008

I Hope

I hope the world around you,
Brings you so much peace and love
I know that you've been angry
But I wanted to share my love.

I hope the people treat you
With tender loving care,
I want for you the very best
Forever and most fair.

I hope the world around you
Directs you along the path
I sense that we have drifted
Wishing you every happiness.

If I could say I'm sorry
For everything I've done wrong
I'd do it in a heart beat
I'd sing it in my song.

So as you exit and leave me
Remember my words to you
I wish you every Blessings
And my heart goes with you too.

I Have Only Me to Give

I have only me to give
I beg you allowing me to live
In your tender care, and know that You're there
For I do humbly adore.

I'm thankful for all that YOU do
For family and friends—quite a few
I've open my heart, and give till I part
For I love YOU ever more.

Some days I break down and cry
For I have much sorrow inside
I give what I can, from all that I am
My gift of my heart I implore.

Your birthday is now soon at hand
What can I give but who I am
I want to give more, so I open the door
Please accept me and understand.

I don't have a gift to give
What can I do, to be worthy of you
In your tender care, I know that you're there,
I've opened my heart, and give till I part,

I give what I can, from all that I am,
I want to give more, so I open the door
I don't have a gift, on your Holy list,
I Love you MY LORD ever more.

Written by: Mara DeRose
Dec. 12, 2008

I Remember

I REMEMBER WHEN I saw you—the first time
And that bashful little way you smiled at me
And you were embarrassed when I asked your name and told you
The first time!

I remember when you kissed me—the first time
The thrill of your soft, sweet lips upon mine
Baby, you were so inviting, loving you was so exciting
When you kiss me
The first time.

I remember when you touched me—the first time
And held me to your body—the first time
The moment when we came together, I knew my love would last forever
I remember when you touched me…
The first time

The sweet love we're been sharing—the fist time
The sweetest everyday—like vintage wine
For the Good times—that we've been knowing
Somehow would keep on a growing
I'm so thankful that there ever was a "first time!"

I remember when you said good-bye, the first time
And I cried and cried for days like a broken hearted lady
The moment when you moved away, I thought I wouldn't live another day
So now I sit and pray for you, like the first time.

I remember Love Songs sung by you,—the first time
And what meaning they held for me—the first time
If I could do it all again my darling
I'd do it just the same again, and love you even more
Than the first time.

The sweet secret we've shared together—the first time
Are all I have left of you in my soul.
And I shall always cherish the memories that I can remember
Until we meet again and I can hold you again—like the first time.

I Saw God's Face

A gentle hand extended
It fits me like a glove
When GOD appeared to me
My soul was lifted in love!

A mystical hand extended
God's love is shinning through
My soul was lifted higher and higher
By God from out of the blue.

I reached for HIM, my Master
I entered into the light,
It was so comfortable and happy
My spirit soared in flight.

Mother Mary then appeared
I felt the Peace surround
No need to ask the questions
For answers were in abound.

Then I opened my eyes again
And felt a longing for HIM
For one day, He will take me
And, bid me enter in?

When I looked upon His face
He was covered in hues
His gown of white was flowing
Peace was long over due.

I saw His face in desperation
I felt the warmth surround
He gestured for me to come to Him
As He placed his arms around.

Joyous laughter began to ring
As the music filled the space
And my heart was filled to the brim
At this wonderful and Holy Place!

I Thank You Father

(Thanksgiving Prayer)

I thank you Father—from the bottom of my soul
I thank you Father, you'll allowed me to grow old
Each day is getting shorter, the nights are growing long
But on This OUR THANKSIGVING—I Praise you with my song.

I thank you Father as my family gathers round
I thank you Father, for one day I'll be heaven bound
Each day I say my Rosary, at night I try and do
All the things you've taught me, and helped to guide me through

I thank you Father, for the gifts you've shared with me
I thank you Father, You are the guardian while I sleep
I ask you now my Father, for all the wars to cease
Find cure for all diseases and shelter to increase.

On this our Thanksgiving Day, I give my heart to you
I offer all I have and gladly give, in everything I do
I thank you Father and pray one day I'll see
You're bidding me to enter, and finally be at peace.

I thank you Father, for my entire family
I thank you Father, and giving what we need
I know you heard my prayers before, and that I ramble on
But Thanking you dear father, will help me to be strong.

I thank You Father for directing my every step
I thank you Father, as the promises you've kept
With autumn weather almost gone, soon time will fly and we'll be gone
You helped me survive in every storm…I praise your name.

Written by: Mara DeRose
Sept. 19, 2008

I Will Be Here for You

I will be here for you, no matter day or night
I will be here for you, when the dark turns light
No matter what you do, I'll be here waiting for you
For my love for you will never end.

I will be by your side, as long as you want
I will confide in you, you make me strong
No matter how long it takes, no matter how much we break
Oh how much give and take, I'll be here for you.

I will be making plans, for you and me love
I will be chasing dreams, when push comes to shove
No matter which way you go, I just want you to know
My love will surely grow…my love.

One day we'll be man and wife my love
So give it a chance my love, for life
No matter if you decide, I hope that I satisfy
On that day your realize, my love.

If

If flowers were people—you'd be a rose
If children were taught to stay on their toes
If fields were filled—summer, winter and fall
Rivers over-flowing in no direction at all.

If clouds were like raindrops all over my face
If souls were ascending to that beautiful place
Cure all of His Children from their disease
If God would soon grant us His heavenly peace?

If only we thanked HIM for all that He's done
We'd have trillions of miracles—and we would be one
If rocks could scatter far away from each wall
There is no need in His Kingdom at all.

If grass were each pathway—the gates open wide
Our Lord would be there to greet us inside
Because heaven has no visible floors
There would be no need for guns, bombs or wars.

If oceans could speak instead of just roar,
If only I meet the ones I adore.
My God and my Savior, Mother Mary I implore
Will you please be there when I come to your door?

If stresses were butterflies—they'd all fly away
If worries were rainbows—they'd dance out each day.
If breezes were symphonies—they'd sing through the trees,
Then wash over my body—sending prayers on my knees.

If I

If I could give you flowers
For every kind thing you've done,
You'd have a bouquet to fill your home
And your rooms would shine in the sun.

If I could give you silver,
For each time you've given your care
You'd have the brightest halo
There'd be no gray in your hair.

If I could give you diamonds
For all the deeds that you've shared
You'd sparkle and shine forever
And God would see you there.

If I could love you better
Than I ever have before
You'd be so happy Auntie,
You'd be dancing round the floor.

If I could sing any better
For the many times you've loved
Your heart would be so happy
You'd be cooing like a dove.

If I could pray any harder
God would open up his heart
And allow us all to enter,
And we'd never more would part.

If I could build you a mansion,
And furnish it to the hilt

You'd have the biggest house then
Can you picture on that hill.

If I could go and greet you
Each time we separate
The world would stop revolving
And heaven would open its gate.

If I could give you tokens
Each and every day that I live
There'd be no room for anything else
Cause you'd have all I own to give.

So on this special day dear
I offer my heart to you
I give you all and more things
Along with my Blessings too.

Happy Mother's Day

I'm Holding My Breath

I'm holding my breath, till I hear my name
I'm waiting to start my moment of fame.
I'm standing here scared, but through it all
I offer my heart, and my THANKS most of all…

I've tried my best, to please each of you,
I've given my heart, and when I was through,
I stood here and took the judgments you gave
I took them so proudly, and so well behaved.

I'm holding my breath, till I hear my name
One moment in time, one moment of fame
I offered my heart, along with my prayer
I give it to you, without any despair

I'm Never Gonna Let You Go

I'm never gonna let you go LORD,
I'm never gonna let you go
You have changed my path Lord
My heart is telling me so
I'm never gonna stop my love LORD
I'm gonna try the best that I can
I'm trying to change who I was Lord
You have given me a brand new plan.

I'm never gonna be alone Lord
You will always be by my side
I feel you all around me
I hope you'll see how hard I've tried
And when I go to sleep Lord
I'll say my prayers as I close my eyes
I want to be a better person LORD,
You make me feel so special inside.

I'm never gonna let you go LORD,
For I want you to be a part of my life
For without you inside me LORD
I couldn't last a day with this strife
And when the final day comes LORD
I hope you'll be there to show me the way
To guide each step through your gates Lord,
And this I do humbly pray…

November 30, 2008

Written by: Mara DeRose

In God's Front Yard

In the yard of God, we see many things
We view the universe before all strings
We search for treasures, under the sun
The moon brings pleasure to everyone.

In God's front yard, we hear the cries
People's desperation, those rising sighs
We observe the need, but do not hasten
We only have wants of desperation.

In God's back front yard, we turn a deaf ear
We wander about through year to year
We have no morals, we have no guilt
We don't give a damn for what we've built.

In God's front yard, we do as we please
Hardly giving thanks upon our knees
We take for granted what He has done
WE never give back to the Holy One.

In God's front yard, ignoring His laws
We travel on, and give no applause
We take whatever comes into sight
Nothing in return...Into our flight.

In God's sweet home, you'd think we'd care
You'd expect more love for us to share
We beg and borrow and steal if we dare
Our hearts won't listen, we lost our fare.

In God's front yard, why do we do
Those things we shouldn't, we must undo

One day will come—the judgment day
We then will bow, to His bouquet

Will I be there in God's front yard
Will I wander around His guard
I want to be in His front yard
I hope and plea, for some reward?

One day will come—soon enough my friend
Until that day…He'll take me in…
Upon that day, in His front yard
His inspection, there is no chard.

In God's front yard, I'll try and see
The stars in the haven beckoning me
As I approach—God's front door
I beg to enter, forever more.

In God's front yard, In God's front home
I pray I won't be all alone
I hope He'll greet me, and find my mirth
I pray and pray, for all I'm worth…

In God's front yard, in God's sweet place
Open your heart, give Him the space
Allow HIM in, and keep up your face
So YOU won't bring Him—any disgrace.

In God's front yard, in God's front yard?

Written by: Mara DeRose
July 28, 2008

In HIS ARMS

In His ARMS, that reach out for you
He'll give you the strength to hold you,
The Grace to sustain you,
and His LOVE to carry you through.
In HIS arms, He will teach you,
When he reaches out to touch you,
And will guide you
into righteousness each day.

So life up your spirit—
in prayer and devotion
Give HIM everything you
offer on this day.
He will provide you—
with all things that sustain you
In His ever-lasting arms…
Let us pray…

Wait on the lord,
and be of good courage
And He shall un-encumber
your hearts
In HIS tender mercies,
Speak to loving actions
And promote us to do our daily part.

Sing Alleluia, praise Him and implore Him
Give Him your adoration, and your deeds
Sing Alleluia, lift up your voices,
Offer Him everything He needs.

Written by: Mara DeRose
April 27, 2008

In My Room

In my room, two shades to hide the real me
Two windows to keep out the free
I'm alone, thoughts that won't let me be
I crave some sleep—it's not turning the key
In my room, in my room, in my room

In my room, my mirror reflects chards of me
Two bureaus that can't possible be
Pictures with fond memories
Tearing at heart strings that see
In my room, in my room, in my room

In my room, there is a big wooden door
There is hard wood on the floor
Shiny and clean, life I want more
I sit and stare from my core
In my room, in my room, in my room.

In my room, clothes that hang on the hook
Gathering dust in the nook
Over there in the corner…a book
Somehow I shutter to look
In my room, in my room, in my room.

In my room, there is a big brass bed
One that is usually covered in red
Spindles reaching over my head
While I sit there and nothing is said
In my room, in my room, in my room.

In my room, the phone rings as I wait
First one—then two…I hesitate

Could it be you, and my fate
Wondering if you'll—find my gate
In my room, in my room, in my room

In my room, all alone with my memory
Waiting and praying to be
The one that will liberate and set free
From all this uncertainty
In my room, in my room, in my room.

In my room, I kneel and I pray everyday
Well into the night, I will stay
Alone in my room, my nerves fray
Hoping God takes it away
In my room, in my room, in my room.

Written by: Mara DeRose
July 29, 2008

I Took a Ride

I took a ride on the Long Island Railroad
And looked out the window at the view
Before I knew it you were seated next to me
My heart was beating faster and I knew

I didn't dare to stare into your deep blue eyes
I held my breath when the conductor came
He asked for our tickets and I touched your hand
I was hoping that you might feel the same...

I heard a melody coming from the tracks
As the train raced on down the line
It was singing out a phrase as it hummed along
That you were the one I wanted all the time.

By the time I reached the station
You got up to leave
And my heart was imploring for a chance
To say all those things that a person should say

Yes, I took a ride of the Long Island Railroad
I lost my heart as well as head
Although our paths never crossed again
I will always remember what was said.

I hear the click clack of the wheels rolling by
I wonder if you ever think of me
I pause when we came into the station and sigh
What an adventure this could be.

It's Almost Christmas Time

It's almost Christmas time again
And hear those Carols sung and then
It's time for Mistletoe and Holly
And for hearts to be oh so jolly
Wrap the gifts with bows and paper
And the gift tags sort of draper
The snow is softly falling
And the wind is sweetly calling
And the logs upon the fire
With the flames creeping higher
We'll all gather round the table
Give our thanks for all we're able
I long to be home just one more time
I'd want to welcome friends of mine
So won't you open up the door
Have one more dance along the floor.

See the children on the hill
Sleighing up and down until
The snowballs start a flowing
Playing games while always knowing
As they build their snowmen high
Almost up to reach the sky
Soon they heading off for rest
Apple cider and cinnamon crest
Soon be off to sleep
Close their eyes and don't they peek
Time to put away all cares
And remember toys and bears
Christmas came and has gone then
Another year has blessed us once again
Another Christmas for you and me.
As we stand beside our Christmas Tree.

It's Your

It's your body language, that sets my soul on fire
It's your lingering glances, that fills me with desire
You're the one that I want only, and you permeate my heart
Look into my eyes and tell me, that we will never part.

It's your conscience connection, to a life that we can share
It's your movements and gestures, that has me soaring everywhere
From the moment I first met you, I felt a undulating pulse
When your wrap your arms around me, and I know that this is love

It's your sense of humor, that created in my mind
It's your love that sustains me, and stands the test of time
We can stroll the earth together, making plans for happiness
We can dance to different rhythms, yet we know that we are blessed.

It's your humanity towards others—that comes shinning through
It's your positive expression, makes me feel the way I do
Day by day on life's highway, taste and seek a love divine,
All I'll give to you a flower that will stand for love so sublime.

I Wished I'd Been There

I wished I had been there when you were crucified
I don't know if I could have stood still as you hung your head and died
You said, "Forgive them Father for they know not what they do!"
But I say, Jesus Christ, you've save us all from the darkness of hell
And I will always love you.

You're dying for our sins of the world, has made me stop and think
I hope someday I can repay, all the sufferings that you did for me?
As you rose up from the dead on that Blessed Easter morn;
Let me sing your praises to the highest this and everyday.
Until we meet at dawn.

I hope I can help spread "YOUR GOOD NEWS" to all those I meet
May you bless me and keep me always at your Holy Feet?
May I feel your healing love everyday you give to me,
May I never forget all the Blessings you've bestowed especially on me.
I love you LORD, AMEN

Journey

Two friends sharing this journey we're riding
Searching for answers to questions hidden
As we travel down this roadway of life
You've helped to release stresses and strife.

You have reminded me time and again
No matter what, You are IMPORTANT—my friend!
You've carried me through darkness into the light.
Coming out of the shell is a mystical flight.

You're real inspiration has provided to me
A heart that is willing to let me soar free.
As you've watched me stumble and fall.
You've picked me up…making me stands so tall.

Life gives us each a terrible thirst.
You're always putting other's needs first.
My heart gives you THANKS, as I walk through the land.
You've opened the door to the journey at hand.

Laughing on the Outside

I'm always Laughing on the Outside,
Crying on the inside,—everyday of my life
I feel so unhappy,—and I'm so very lonely
Since you've been gone.

I'm not able to go on giving
When the reason for my living—has found another to love
I'm laughing on the outside—Crying on the inside,
since you've said "so long"

I feel so rejected, and still I had suspected
Things were not right for sometime
And I'm Laughing on the outside, Crying on the inside
Since you left me alone.

I'd give anything to have you back again
In my arms and in our home
So I'll be laughing on the outside, crying on the inside
Please baby won't you come on home?

Everyday when I awake
and your not here beside me
I have an awful ache,
and I'm longing to hold you near

I know I can't continue
living my life this way
So, I'll be laughing on the outside,
crying on the inside
Every solitary day.

Life Happens

In each life there's a beginning, middle and an end
We all have our journey, along with so many bends
We have our secret moments, and we also have the trends
Life happens without us realizing, we are headed towards the end.

As we travel along God's highways,
we are searching for health and happiness
We go along willy nilly, and we dream of our success
Can we expect anything less…????

Life Happens when we are grinding out
Each day and not looking around
For all those roses in our path
And all the seas that life surrounds.

In each life there's a beginning, a Middle, and an end…
We have our special journey, and a lot of fences to mend.
We hope we do not offend our Lord, we ask for tender care
We don't know how long we have, but we hope that He'll be there…

Written by: Mara DeRose
March 22, 2007

Life Isn't Fair

Life isn't fair at times, but
LIFE surely is a gift
God granted us upon our birth
And we must hold on to HIS Wish.
Life isn't fair when it comes to
Where we are born and to whom
We do not have a choice whose our MOM
But we learn to follow God's rule.

Life is beautiful, life is valiant
Life can be harsh and unkind
Life can be cruel and we cant' understand
WE travel though not knowing "it's rhyme"
Make each day you write upon
Be memorable, be helpful and caste
For we do not know what tomorrow will bring
We don't know how long it will last.

When Life is treating you so unfair
And you have no answers in mind
Just turn to the one who created it all
And allow HIM to ease all in sign
Turn to Him, trust in Him
For He knows what's best
Life can be fair if we give HIM our needs
I know God will do all the rest.

Written By: Mara DeRose
November 14, 2008

Little Squirrel, Little Squirrel

Little Squirrel, little squirrel
High up in the tree
Sunning yourself on a tree trunk
Can't tell if you can keep
Little Squirrel, little squirrel
You are fast asleep
I can sit here and watch you—
While you hide and seek.
I wonder if God is watching over you
Is that your little friend?
I see him jumping back and forth
And each and every bend.
He is looking to protect you.
Just as God did for you and me
I wonder if you are hungry—
I wonder what will be?
Little squirrel, little squirrel
I wished I could do more
Than throw you some sunflower seeds
Don't fall on God's green floor.

Little Squirrel, Little squirrel
I love to watch you leap
You scale the lively tree stems
No place for you to sleep
Little squirrel, little squirrel
I thought I saw a tree knot
But you were there so still
Until you had y our fill.
Little squirrel, little squirrel
Soon it's time to hibernate
Then old winter's song will hum
And snow will cover up the gate!

Looking in a Mirror

When I look into a mirror,
What do I perceive?
I see a mysterious woman
Staring back at me.

When I glance into a mirror,
What do I feel?
I feel such loneliness,
I wonder how this can be.

When I see my own reflection
What do I want?
I want to be whole-heartedly loved
Can this ever be?

When I gaze into my being
What do I assume?
God will lift me up
Raising me to another room

When I resolve to do my best
What do I desire?
I chose great love
To set my soul a fire.

When I sense the woman before
What do I consider?
Will His ambiance reach?
And will I be delivered?

Looking in my mirror,
What do I expect?
Answers too many questions
And complete my happiness?

When I am hungry for the truth,
And my mirror allows me to see
Am I the woman in the mirror?
Staring back inside of me?

My mirror never lies
It shows me as I am
The foreigner even unto myself
Put upon His Holy Land.

My mirror reflects the truth
As strange as it may seem,
It's a very disturbed image
And it's my over-flowing stream.

Chards of luminous light
In the prisms in the outline
Pictionary of a spirit
And a body on the incline…

Looking in my mirror
Reflections of my "now"
Voyage of my lifetime
Seems rather strange somehow.

March 19, 2005

After a period of weakness I light headed I laid down for awhile.
I woke up and then decided to say my Rosary so I lit a candle cause I just couldn't sleep. That's when I started the Rosary and then I heard the voice of Mother Mary. She told me, "You must take care of Bobby as he's sicker than I am! Don't be frightened daughter, Trust in Him, my Son." He is there with you now, let HIM come in! Rest assured you'll be okay...Now go and lay down for awhile and sin no more. I have heard you in prayer. Now go lay down Pray, pray for those who are in need of ME just pray,
"I will Mother Mary" I will do as you have asked."
She wanted me to do this each time I said my prayers
"Light the candle and pray.
"Oh Mary conceived without sin, pray for me!"
"Each time you say it—it will calm you down."

She also said that Pope John Paul would die in three days
Your father will understand one day
You are forgiven your trespasses
You may tell your family.
Pray for Peace and Peace will be granted soon
Continue to pray for all the things you have been praying for all along.
You may write this down so you will remember
Put the time here 9:34 PM
"My son suffered for you and all his children." "Thank HIM!"
"Say an act of contrition and now and go to sleep
Go to the doctor tomorrow morning
Wear my Medal. Continue to pray—now rest."

I'm much too excited to sleep Mother"

"You need to rest, I will come to you again."

"Thank you Mother Mary!"
I love you, Your Son, St. Joseph and the Holy Trinity

"After you said your prayers—blow out the candle!"

I wrote this all down from the pages in my notebook that it truly happened just as I've written here. I do believe that Mother Mary's voice came to me and spoke the words above, and I swear it on my life. I'm writing down here on the computer so one day we can look back and remember her words to me because I'm getting to that point where I can't remember things. I will continue to pray to Mary and do my Rosary each day. I Hope that it will be good enough for PEACE to come to the world, Cures for all diseases, Pope John Paul, For the souls in Purgatory, For my family, friends and all those who've asked me to pray for them. Also for the unborn babies and their Mother's that they won't have any abortions, I also pray for Conversions of sinners, for more HOLY MEN and Women to join the priesthood and Religious life.

While saying the Rosary during each section I recite "Oh Mary Conceived without Sin, Pray for us who have recourse to thee. 3 times each decade.

I am waiting to see if Pope John Paul dies in three days before I allow anyone to know what's happened to me. I don't want John Paul to die on Tuesday, but it's not up to me. I will continue my prayers for HIM too.

Oh God, in your Divine Mercy please let this be a message from your Holy Mother and not the devil's work. I ask you this through your Son, Jesus Christ, who lives and reigns with you and the Holy Spirit, one God forever, and Ever Amen.

Help me do HIS WILL and not that of my own.

Amen!

Written by Maralyn DeRose
A true account of my day and prayer.

I swear by all that's HOLY!

Mary's Child

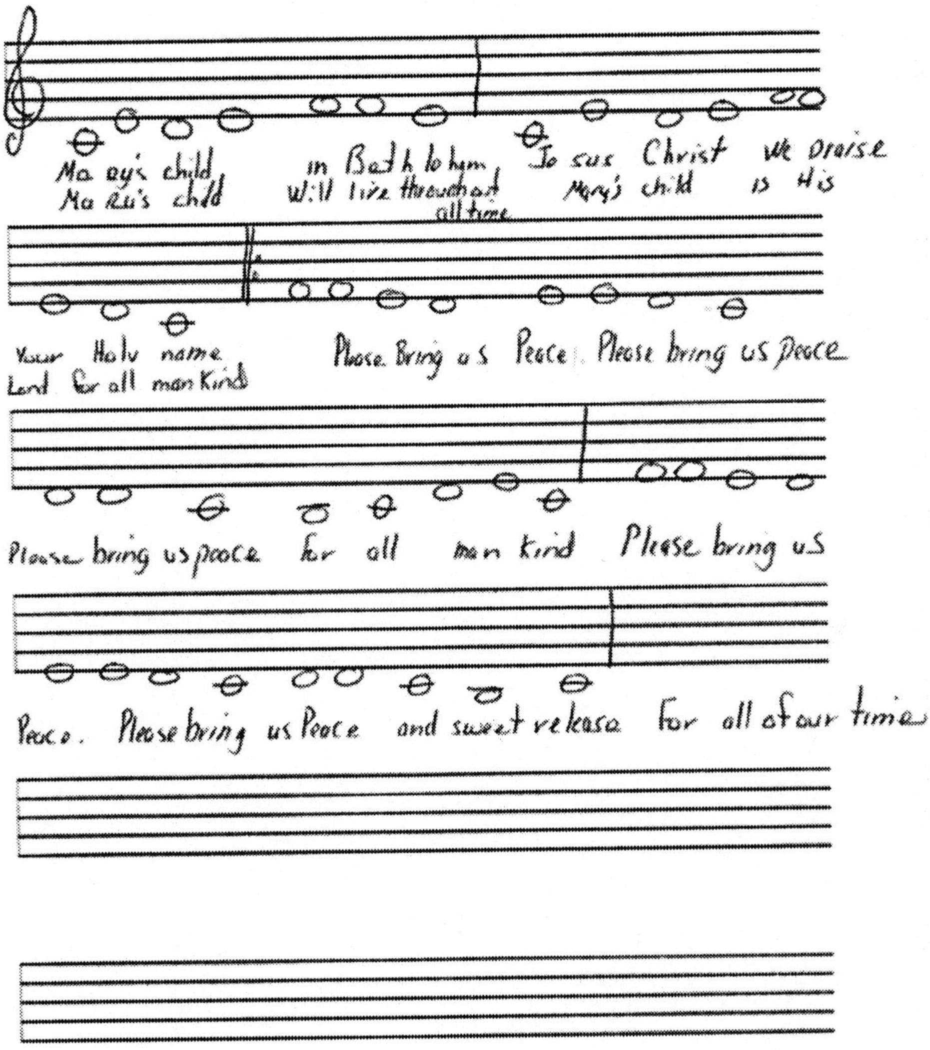

Ma ry's child in Beth le hem Je sus Christ we praise
Ma ry's child Will live throughout all time Mary's child is His

Your Holy name
Lord for all man kind

Please Bring us Peace. Please bring us peace

Please bring us peace for all man kind Please bring us

Peace. Please bring us Peace and sweet release for all of our time

Melody So Sweet

As I saunter down the rocks
Right up to the ocean's edge
I place my toes into the sand
Where seaweed has made a bed.

The water weaves in and out
A Melody oh so sweet
I hear the cries of seagulls
As I walk along the beach.

In my solitude as I walk
The seashells on the floor
Has opened up a space for me
To walk along its shore.

The wind whips up the water
Into a graceful dance
It forms so many sparklettes
Its hypnotic motion puts one in a trance.

Splashing up against huge boulders
As the tides ebb in and out
It's a garnish of water exploding
As the boats are tossed about.

The tranquil sounds that waves do make
Is PEACEFUL to my ears
When I am down trodden
I remember through my tears.

The specks of sand that clings
To my toes and along my soles

I will long remember
When my youngness turns me old.

The ocean still beacons me
To come and share "the still"
I try and am available
And I guess I always will.

So if you go down to the water
And allow yourself to feel
Listen for the melody
And allow yourself to heal…

As I ponder my thoughts
And recall my day at the shore
I will forever be
A part of the great outdoors.

I love the melody oh so sweet
And I guess I'll always hear
It's such an awesome treat
It gets me through each year.

Memorial to DAD

Go lay you down DAD—go lay you down,
Go lay you down DAD your family surround
You can find rest DAD on tender earth
Go lay you down DAD in your rebirth

Hear the birds caw DAD—smell blossoms in bloom,
Open your heart dad, soar out of the room
The birds in the tree tops, are singing in tune
Go lay you down DAD. You have plenty of room.

Now as I leave you, I turn away
Over the years Dad How I have prayed
One day you'd notice how I have changed
I'll come to visit again and again.

Go lay you your head down, you need your rest,
I thank you Father, I pray He'll be blessed,
Go join my Mother, give her a kiss,
Tell her I miss her, that is my wish.

Go Lay you down DAD, slumber in Peace,
I am here waiting the grass 'neath my feet,
I'll pray for you Dad—my father, and friend,
Go lay in death DAD, your road is at hand.

Go lay you down Dad, Lay your head down
Lay down and rest now, 'neath hallowed ground,
I will remember, all the days of my life,
How I do miss you, my father for life!

Written by : Mara DeRose
Updated April 17h, 2008

Memories

Memories they come and go
Why they come, I do not know
They sprinkle shadows on my brain
I ponder about this; am I insane?

Flashes of darkness, into the light
Instructing me to relive the sight
Did I do what I wanted? Was it right?
This day will be out of site…

Days come and days go
And still I am here
I wonder why; I question where
Why is it that I'm filled with fear?

Memories of happy, some of sad
Sounds that make me OH so glad
Invades my soul with purpose unclear
Will I still be here at the end of the year?

Dancing around in my brain over time
Weaving it's spell, taking it's rhyme
Cascading over the waves deep inside
I am here, along for this ride

Restoration of my sanity
Kaleidoscope of feelings be,
Rejuvenates my heart for all to see
Memories why are you asserting me?

Mother I Miss You

Mother, how I miss you
Are you with the Angels now?
Will you wait for me to join you?
Will you take my hand somehow?

Will you guide my troublesome footsteps?
Will you watch me as I come and go?
Can I share with you my treasures?
Shall we pass and never show?

Mother, how I miss you
Each day is lost without too
Some days are difficult crosses to bear
But I feel you will enlighten me with care!

Can you say Hello to Grandma?
Will you give her a little hug?
Will you tell her that her daughter
Is my heart, my hand, my love?

Mother how I miss you
You will never know
Wait for me my dearest,
And never let me go—

Take my heart to GOD now,
Ask him if I may enter in?
Wait for me dearest Mother
We will reunite again.

Oh dear Mother how I miss you
I think of you every day
I feel your presence around me
I miss you more than words can ever say.

Mother-in-Law

Everyone says you're my Mother in law
But you mean much more to me;
You have taken a special place in my heart
And I love you, as you can see?
Over the years we've come to know
The trust we share with each day
We feel one another's pain
I wished I could take yours away?
You are unique in your love you share
And you love me unconditionally
Some days are hidden behind dark clouds
But you chase them away for me.
March now sings its usual song
Of days too short and too long
My music makes a merrier sound
Especially when I know you're around.
You have given so freely of yourself
Each day is a new experience
I look forward to our chats at night
As if we were in a dance.
In prayer I seek the answers today
I ask God to hold you near
There is no distances can keep us away
This I have no fear.
So be my friend, my mentor, my MOM,
Be all of these things and much more
Always know that you are in my heart
And will remain there forever more.

Mother Mary

The beauty of a rose cannot compare
To your loving face of a Mother so rare
Smile down upon your people Mother most Holy
Grant us His Peace, and won't you please show me?
The beauty of a rose so delicate and fragrant
As my prayers ascends knowing how my day went.

The beauties within hearts is truly open
Gifts of HIS SPIRIT come to us—I'm hoping?
For I'm waiting for your GRACE—through YOUR SON
It will make this day complete—my heart has won
BODY AND BLOOD from bread and wine
Blessed by GOD—His love is so divine.

Mother of Mine

Today I remember the light in your eyes
The smile on your lips and the calming disguise
I think of you during happier days
Your caring heart,—your wonderful ways
It's your birthday today, and I'm thinking of you
Knowing that tears—can't bring me to you
I wished I could take back each tear and each frown
To turn back the clock and make it go round
For I miss you so much since God whisked you away
Oh how I wished I could make up today
Relieve you of stresses that you surely had
And give you back to my father and DAD
You are now in heaven, angels holding your hand
Sprinkle all memories, upon your grave stand
My heart filled with love and memoirs too
Oh how I love you, and miss you…I do!

Written by: Mara DeRose
July 14, 2000

My Chance

Tonight, my dream has come true
I have the chance to dream bigger than I ever could
I'm on the brink of a brand new life
And the chance to obtain if I could

Tonight, I won't disappoint your gifts
I'll give all I can till there's nothing left to give.
I'll sing till my voice can't sing any more
And I'll give my best, till you ask for more…

Tonight, my dream is to win
The hearts and the minds of my friends
I offer my songs and my gifts
Until I have nothing more to give…

My Dearest

The passion that I'm feeling in my pounding heart won't cease
Release the hunger that is imprisoned within my soul.
Eagerly I await the sound of your voice.
It quickens my every breath as I sit silently with my heart up in my mouth
Oh sweet melodies ramble across my subconscious in chanting whispers.
You are my life, my heart, my mind.
Somewhere, I suspect, deep within your very being you'll agree
That love is a true love, and you feel those same feelings for me?
So touch me, kiss me, make love with me, I only want to be with you.
All this I offer you from all I have—I've been all I ever will be.
You are my Passion, my soul, my heart.
That is why I wake up in the middle of each night and reach for you—
You are not there, am I dreaming?
What will become of me?
Only you hold the keys to unlock this melody of time and space.
Answer my love, and I shall be ever with you until the sun rises and sets
For the last time upon these tired eyes.

Ecstasy is but just a moment away from your touch.
Reach out and take of me what you will
I will not challenge your moves
You will take and drink of me what you will and never regret
The moments that have passed between us
Like ebbing tides, so the movement of this dance
We do will meld away those inhibitions you once held so dear.
And You will be consumed with the fire that ignites your body as your flesh would come ever nearer to its goal.
Again, I say to you—take what you will and hold me close—for thine is mine and I will not have it any other way.

Loving you has been the most precious gift that one person can give to another

The fact that I have bestowed it upon you, says a lot in itself
You must decide what will be—either nay, or yeah—but not lost in the thought
That you give to one and not the other, for neither can be done.
You will let me be all—or nothings—what more can be said?

My Family

My family all begins with the Holy Trinity
My family is mostly you and a little of me
When I'm down on my knees to pray—I pray to Jesus everyday
That He will bless us from above' and send this old world all His LOVE.
My family—all began so long ago
My family—is when I learned to love Him so
He sent me many gifts—I'm sure
And one sweet gift—that will endure
Is My Family-and what you all mean to me.

My family—is my sweet Jesus on that tree
My family is my church where I can see
The love that circles all around—the love that comes to all our minds
Never ceases, nor decreases only fills our soul's with grace
When we'll see Him face to face

My family—filled with hope instead of tears
My family—has lasted all these years
Forgive us from our daily sins; help us when we pray to HIM
Give us bread and wine to drink to make us always stop and think

My family—is as warm as it can be
My family—is the Blessed Trinity
When I lay me down to sleep—The Good LORD is always watching over me
Even tho' I shall arise...Lord please listen to the cries of this—My family!

My family—is my Holy Rosary
My family is my prayers to Mother Mary
Without her Son sent from above
I'd have never known her love. My Family!

My God

In every facet of my life
I am a multifaceted foundation
I have unquenchable dreams
I am God's creation.

Life appointments that I fulfill today,
Are those of my own choosing?
I volunteer my love
To those who surround my reason.

Soothe my mind in these dastardly days
And bring me to new understanding
Take away from this valley in haze
A bright new tomorrow I maybe confronting.

Inspire my steps to blaze a new travel
I leap but I feel I am falling.
I look for a new ideal and vision
I answer to a "higher" calling.

And soon my life will be over and done,
What have I contributed to man?
Just a soul that has given her all
To THANK the Lord for this span!

Remove the blackness of a death,
And open sunshine—always bending
Enter in upon "holy ground"
With a love that is never ending.

My God, My God

My God, My God, I am in need of your Mercy
I am so tired of living in sin,
I wished I could rest without guilt

My God, My God, I love you my friend
I am so tired of my life this way
I wished I could chance my ways.

My God, My God, take me by the hand
Show me the way to reclaim
My life is nothing without you.

My God, My God, take pity on me
Even though I know I don't deserve it
Point me towards the peaceful garden?

My God, My God, watch over my family
Let them know how much I love them
And how much I care every hour…

My God, My God, hear my heart speak
For without you I have nothing
I am lost inside my head.

Witten by: Mara DeRose
January 13, 2008

My GOD, I'm Asking You

My God, My God I am asking you to hear
My prayer in humility, my prayer in despair
My God, My God, I feel so all alone
I am waiting to hear, speak to me from your throne

My God, My God, I'm pleading with YOU
To bring peace to earth, and cures for us too
The world around me is in such a mess
I wonder if you hear, all the distress?

My God, My God, I'm trying my best
To share what I have—allowing you to do the rest.
I offer whatever you want me to give
I offer my heart and my soul as I live.

My God, My God, please hear me today
Send forth the angels, sent them, I pray.
There are many suffering, children in pain
What could I do, to help ease their strain?

My God, My God please hear me in prayer
I don't know what to do, in all this despair
My God, My God, I try my very best
Now it's up to YOU LORD, Please do the rest.

My god, My God, the world's in a mess
Send forth your angels, send them down S.O.S.
Global warming, economy is bad
People not working, and housing is sad

My God, My God, what can I do?
My poems reflect all the anguish, for you

My God, My God, I can't take it much more
I need you to answer, you're the one I implore.

My God, My God, please help us today
Send down your answers to questions, I pray
Heal all the sick, and cures for disease
Help all the homeless, so they won't freeze

My God, My God, I'm alone with my prayer
I am praying my best, cause I know you are there
My God, My God, I'm begging of you
I'll do whatever you need me to do.

My God, My God, I'm weak and I'm lazy
I'm fat and I'm lonely, and it's driving me crazy
My God, My God, wash me clean of my sin
Mold me and shape me, and bring me within.

My God, My God, watch over my kin
Guide them and keep them pure from all sin
My God, My God, do miracles today
I'm waiting to hear, as I knee down to pray.

Written by: Mara DeRose
February 13, 2009

My DAD

My heart is heavy with my love
For my father, friend and DaD,
I don't know what to say most times
And sometimes I wished I had.

I try and try with all my strength,
To honor and do what I can
I'll try—I'd go to any length
For a truly, wonderful man.

Days are growing shorter,
And not much time remains,
To say what's in this heart
And not let it unrestrained.

And I offer this to you
Each day is a gift to unwrap
Because my heart is open
And my offer is untapped.

I offer a hand, and a wish
For each day to be the best
Because you are loved dearly
Let your heart do all the rest?

So you are wished this day
"Happiness" for life to share
And open up the dialogue
And let me know you care.

This is your chance to change things
For times that could be again

I pray that you will try
I know I will dear friend.

Let's try and talk and listen
To what each other has to say
And know that we've done all we could
To keep our love today?

MY Grand-Doggie Checkers

When I woke up one morning, creeping across my chest
I saw a pair of big brown eyes, and a black and white curly chest
Two big floppy ears, and a beard of snowy white
That washed my face with kisses, which filled me with delight.

This fluffy doggie gave me love, as she gave me a greeting sweet
I stared back into her eyes, a face and four big feet.
I said, "Good morning Checkers! How are you today?"
She lifted up her paw to me, and she wanted to play.

She pranced around my body and walked around my head
She made me feel responsible, so I climbed out of my bed.
She ran towards the hallway, following behind the back of my knees
I knew exactly what she needed…to walk her under the trees.

We walked and talked, she tugging me, stopping along the way
She sniffed and sniffed the grasses, as if she had to say
I'll make Pee and Poo for you, and then we'll hurry back
If you'll give me a "Greenie" as a very special snack?"

I filled her bowl with water,
And piled the food into her bowl
She sniffs and sniffs at the food that's there
But not a morsel does she console.

I try and sneak back upon my bed, to take a little nap
Checkers has other ideas, while jumping on my back.
My eyes are heavy as I fall back to sleep
Checkers follows me, into a deep long sleep.
She thinks that she's a person

And I heartily agree,
For she is my Grand-doggie
Though a doggie she maybe.

Written by: Mara DeRose

My Little Gift

Although you cannot see my gift
Which didn't cost a thing
It does not have decorations
So it doesn't sparkle or bling.

Although my gift I give to you
I thought just for you today
I'd give to you my dearest friend
My hand, my heart as I pray.

It doesn't make a sound or glow
And when it's opened up
You cannot eat or drink it
Or put it in a cup.

Please accept my little gift
I offer now to you
My gift is here inside my heart
It's my respect and love for you.

My Love for Food

Crusty, spiraled kneaded bread
Savory, swirled crunchy spread
Meltingly tender classical roll
Pungent, tangy, laid in a bowl.

Rustic, herbal, shredded cheese
Sugary, syrup, honey-filled sleeves
Roasted, crushed, aromatic delights
Nutty, salted, buttery in bites.

Flavorful, palatable, delectable treat
Lip smacking, appetizing, mouthwatering feat
Succulent, scrumptious, braised on the top
Juicy, mélange, wrapped in a broth.

All these things are my love for food
I wonder if I can conclude
That my body craves things I don't need
My Love for food I shall concede

My Man

Many words of love have been written before
But this song that I sing is for one I adore
My Man, I've built my whole life around
And by his side, is where I'll be found.

By the song that I sing—you can tell that I care
By the song that I sing, you know I've been there
By the song that I sing, you can tell I'll be true
By the song that I sing, you'll know I love you.

When he comes home from work each night
He kisses me gently and holds me so tight
Caresses my hair, and then takes my hand
He needn't ask: He knows what I've planned.

We'll spend this night lost in our dreams,
Till the sun comes alive, with dazzling beams
When we wake, he turns off the alarm
And we lay so quiet; me in his arms.

By this song that I've sung, you heard me say
I'll love you forever—till my dying day
But this song that I've sung has come to and end
So "Hello" my lover, my sweetheart, my friend.

Negativity

My Car isn't workin'
My headache is jerkin
And my Bills are not being paid

The roof is still leaking
My job search is bleak and
The mortgage is in foreclosure stage.

The leaves are still blowin'
The piles are still growing
I've no one to cart them away.

My stomach is growling
The winds are a howling
My face gets a gusting bouquet.

And squirrels are contesting
The birds are through nesting
Their flight to the south any day

The garbage cans rolling
And papers are flowing
The wind is just thrashing away.

No sense in complaining
When sun turns to raining
WE live one more day to pray.

Negativity

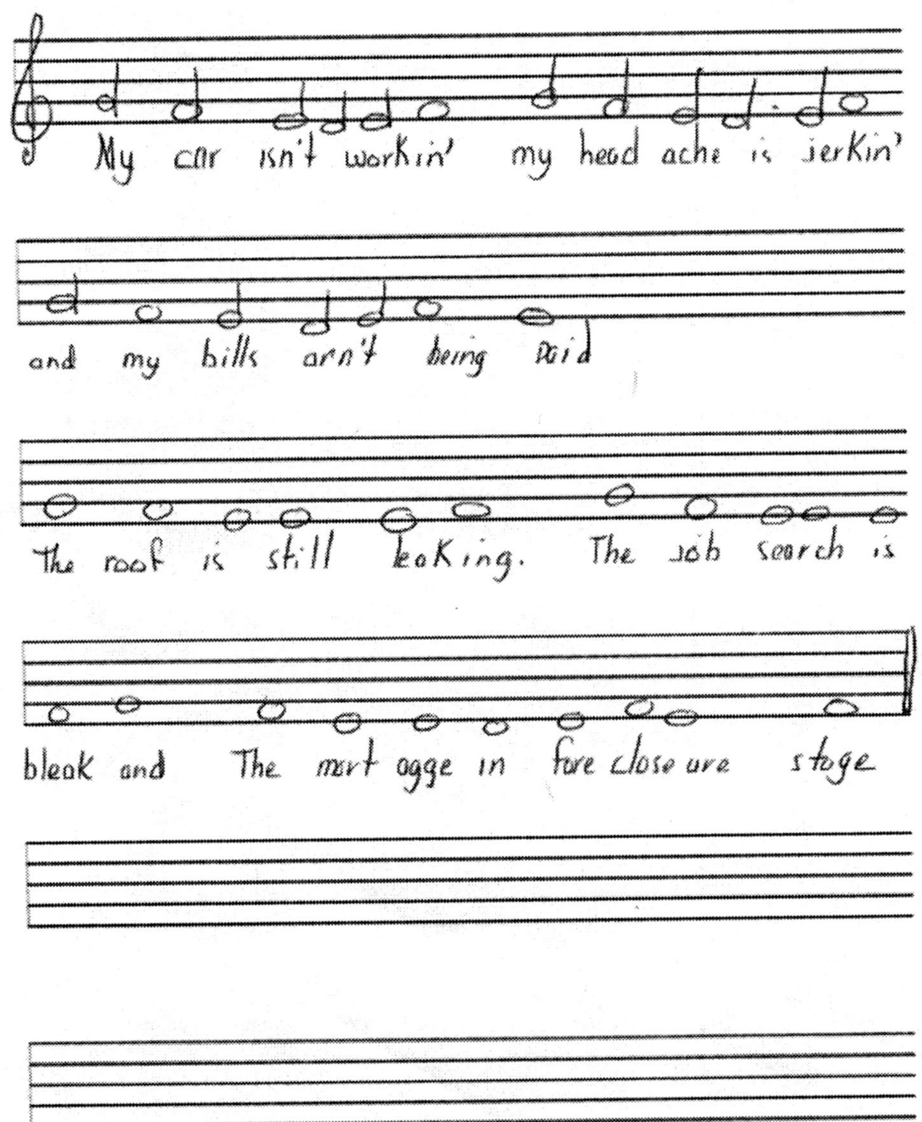
My car isn't workin' my head ache is jerkin'
and my bills arn't being paid
The roof is still leaking. The job search is
bleak and The mort gage in fore close ure stage

Nighttime

When the nighttime reclines from the sky
When it becomes a face in a flower
There is no rest for the weary
There is no sleep o're the bower

When nighttime waits for the daylight
And doesn't stop just to cower
It veils away in the quiet
And it's journey is ticked by each hour

When the nighttime shoots the stars
Into a cosmic universal shower
And the planets revolve around
And the moon shines through the tower.

As the dawn—displacing the dark
And the shadows recede by the hour
WE face an entire new day
For God has the ultimate power.

No One Like YOU

I've never known anyone quite like you before
I've been truly Blessed since you walked in my kitchen door
How could I ever want for anything, when you've been sweet and kind
God sent you to me, all my Blessings have combined.

I've never known anyone quite like you before
You've given so much help to me my blessings are galore
You've stepped in and took my hand, and did what you do best
You've given in your selflessness, and God did all the rest.

I've never known anyone quite like you before
God has put you in my life, and I couldn't ask for more
Each time you come to visit, Your take and do my work
For your love is never ending, and your task you never shirk.

I've never known anyone quite like you before
Your friendship means so much, my trust soars forever more.
And in this time of need you do whatever needs to be done
I can never repay your deeds, but I know Kingdom come.

God sees the good that you have done He's proud as he can be
For you have given so much love, in your charity
And when the day is over, and you need a friend in me
I hope one day I can repay…and bring you clarity.

Now my heart does give you thanks for all you've said and done
Please know how special you are my friend, you are the only one
In my prayers each night I say my holy Rosary
I will thank our God above for giving YOU to me.

Written by: Mara DeRose
October 23, 2008
Dedicated to Rosa Perdomo My Friend

Oh Jesus, Sweet Loving Jesus

March 18, 2009, 11:53 PM

After watching the movie called "The Passion: I am inspired to write this song that Jesus has put into my heart and head…

Oh Jesus, sweet Jesus you died on the cross for me
Oh, Jesus, sweet loving Jesus, you died on the cross for me.

Oh Savior, my sweet loving savior, you died giving me new life
Oh Savior, sweet loving savior, by giving up your life…

Oh Jesus, sweet Jesus, you died on the cross for us
Oh Jesus, sweet loving Jesus, you died on the cross for us.

You surrendered your body and blood so freely
You watched as all those around jeered
And your blood was ever flowing
As your Mother stood and watched in fear.

Forgive us, Jesus forgive us for we know very well what we do
Forgive us, Jesus forgive us, we are sorry for putting you through.

Oh Jesus, sweet loving Jesus, have mercy upon all our souls
Oh Jesus, merciful Jesus, into your Hands we commit our goal.

Oh Jesus, my sweet Jesus, our day will soon come along
Oh, Jesus, I offer my soul, I give it to you in my song.

You were nailed upon the cross for all to see
Give Witness to the truth
And as I recall in my teachings as a child
I offer it all back to YOU…

OH Jesus, sweet loving, I'm singing this song to you
Oh Jesus, sweet loving Jesus, until my time on earth is through.

Written by: Mara DeRose

Old Age & Death

Old age robs us of highways to travel
For dreams are pushed aside replaced with pain
But I trust in God to travel with me
With HIS promise I will someday rise again.

For the pathway—He wants me to follow,
One day soon, I will be place inside the earth
For the grave is very long and shallow
And my soul will know it's true worth.

Wrinkled hands, withered bodies, and loss of hearing
Un-sturdy gait, loss of vision be the "norm,"
Death will soon come a calling
Leaving those left behind to weep and mourn.

Old age takes away strength, mind and beauty
Leaving suffering, egos and uncertainties
God will raise us up from death and duty?
The body dies and allows the soul to soar free.

Grant me Peace, serenity and forgiveness from my sin,
Chant my prayer, my request; while still on earth
Let me pass unto death in sleep-time
Helping me, as well as others, to know our worth!

On the Day We Were Wed

On the day we were wed, I remember,
When I got out of bed, I trembled
I was scared, so were you
But we vowed and said "I do"
And on that day we became one flesh.

On the day we were wed, I can recall
Over forty four years I hear you call
Each day when we arise,
I have tears still in my eyes
But I know that we are one Flesh.

On the day we were wed, I can't forget
When we stood before Our Savior heaven blessed
My heart began to pound
My feet were glued into Hallowed ground
And on that day we became one flesh.

On the day we were wed, was a cold day
But your heart along with mine melted it away
When I saw you standing there
And I knew we'd always care
And on that day we became one flesh.

On the day we were wed, I vowed to be
The best mother around for all to see
Then the day did come along
Our son came and was so strong
And on that day we became one flesh.

Then one day a daughter came to us
She was beautiful and put up such a fuss.

And we knew we've added to our tree.
Now we had our family
And on that day we became one flesh.

Now as I look back upon those years of that day
How I pray that God won't take it all away
For I love you so my friend
As I pray it will never end.
But I know one day we'll meet in heaven someday.

Now my heart is seeking words, trying to say
That I love you more deeply, as time slips away
And I hope you feel the same
And the embers begin to flame
And we celebrate our anniversary my friend!

This is my gift I give to you
I will love and cherish you—the way I do.
If you could only hear
The memories echoing in my ear
I'm your bride for life until the end.

Written by: Mara DeRose
November 22, 2008

ARE WE on the Brink?

Are we on the brink of the end?
Are we going to parish?
I see the dams flood, and over flow their banks
Carrying houses away, people are devastated
The earth is warming, the climate is "hot"
The gas is depleting, it's costing a lot
Children go hungry, when they go to sleep
The earth is in places, barren and weeps

We are still trying to learn what to do
Won't you Please Help us, we're lost without YOU?
Our weather is so harsh, the lightening does flash
The hurricanes leave us, with such after-math,
The oceans are rough now, and come crashing in
It over flows seashores, bringing dangers within.
See all the people scurry around
They need some answers, to all their surround

Sickness and shelters, there are none to be had
This makes my heart feel lonely and sad.
Tornadoes and wind storms, water everywhere
Cries in the night in all our despair
God in YOUR Mercy, answer our pleas?
Bring aid to your world, for we are in need
Are we on the brink, or at an end
It's such a hard question
What's around the next bend?

On the Day I Was Born

On the day I was born, God had given to me
A life before me, that's totally free,
He put in my hands, work health and play
Each day that came forth, in total display
On the day I was born, God had a great plan
To spread before me all over His Land
A heart that is true, and inspiring to sing
And all of the best that a soul could bring.

On the day I was born, God gave me a chance
To write upon each day, and steps for my dance
He put before me a work that I'd love
It was sent from HIS heart with courage above.
On the day I would marry, and have children two,
A boy and a girl, not too many or few.
At home with a garden, and oh what a view
And live till a senior, with worries now due.

On the day I was born, an angel appeared
To watch over and guide me, when trouble was reared.
She'd help me to see, and help me to know
That there were consequences, wherever I'd go.
So I prayed and made peace With my God in my heart
And I vowed to be good and just play my part
And I struggle with pain, and I am such an age
I offer my life, now at the end of my page.

On the day I was born, with parents so rare
They gave what they could, over all of my year
They nurtured me, and gave all they could
Without ever asking, if I really should
My brothers and sister, all care about me
And have added so much to our family tree
Now that I'm aged, and wait for my rest
I am often a visitor, or welcome guest

Our Bodies Will Decay

I know that one day, our bodies will decay
But on that very day, I can only hope pray
That my spirit will carry on, in the hearts of those who mourn
Until that day will come, I believe in His kingdom come.

I know that one day, our lives will somehow end
And our souls will soon ascend
That He's made us a new home, and we'll never ever roam
Until that day does come, I believe we'll still be one.

I know that one day soon, we'll be parted from the room
And we'll never have to seek, as our souls will soon be freed
From the worries and the cares, and from all the worldly cares
And that will be the day, when our hearts will sing and pray.

I know and I believe, that my God is great indeed
And I'll sing to Him my praise, and I'll give Him all my days
I'll turn to HIM with glee, knowing he's forgiven me.
That day will come for sure, and I'll be spirit and adore.

I sense it in my heart, we are coupled and can not part
As My Lord united us on that day, It was on our wedding day
And our children will live on, searching for a brand new dawn
And they will do us proud, and bring Him their Thanks out loud.

So today as I will live, I have my heart to give
And my soul is yours to keep, I will never let it sleep
As my spirit will live in praise, giving thanks along with praise
I am grateful for this time, and I hope I've been kind.

Alleluia—Alleluia Amen

Peggy "O"

Symphony Of The Sea

The sun now closing her eyes for her rest
As waves roll in upon natures best
It splashes and splurges around Old Peggy "O"
The spray flies so high and washes it's toll.
The symphony you hear as she washes ashore
Cascades up each bank, recedes to the floor
With grinding and plunging into the deep
A moments pause erupts from the sleep
Navigating through boulders ad cracks in the wall
You wonder how it's standing facing each squall
Ah the beauty and splendor of the sun lying down
At dusk when the sea is abandoned from the tourists abound
So many stories and tales have been shared
Over the years she's given up her dead
Ah but my heart sings when I peruse the site
My heart beats much faster as she sleeps for the night.
It's home to some seagulls, that dare to fly
They soar seeking droppings from tourists—then fly
Up over this majesty of dear Peggy's place
Then lifts up her daylight and gush the space
Oh Peggy I miss you and your prevalent lights
That shines through the portals both day and night
The hues of red fingerlings of clouds over head
You soon will cover and rest her sweet head
Still there's no sleep for the ocean either day or night
It still crashes and sprays in the dance that delights
No rest for the weary, no rest for the sea,
No rest for the fishes lying under her knee

Perhaps

Perhaps I shall come to an inner peace,
And discovery optimum release
From Physical and emotional pain
Furious humming in my brain.

Perhaps I can mediate
Affirming life as it radiates
Protective presence in my life
Guiding each and every flight.

Nurturing love, constantly flowing
Wonder where I am going?
Complex feelings reaching for harmony,
I honor all diversity

Common factors in each motion
A conquer all with my devotion
Perhaps with time comes prosperity
As I set sail, across the sea.

Magnification of my soul
Ability to light the world as a whole
Encouragement and probability
Perhaps on e day will rejuvenate me

Perhaps my faith deeply rooted within
Gestures of love, laughter and sin
Perhaps will permeate my entire life
And eradicate all my worries and strife.

Psychological Nourishment

When on those days I'm feeling low
I hear some amazing things
I turn again to my Father in Heaven
He grants me everything

When I am in need of love and care
I think and I pray as I feel
I turn to my Father in Heaven again
He shows me the way to be real.

Psychological nourishment
Is what I am in great need
He lifts me to a higher place
And he fills my soul indeed.

Now when one of my friends are sick
And I want to bring them a meal
I offer HIS psychological Nourishment
And then they begin to heal.

Written by: Mara DeRose
June 13, 2005

Questions

Ever notice a squirrel climbing a tree
Hear the birds twittering on a fence
Or sniff the ocean's salty breeze?
Sit on a familiar park bench

Did you watch the ants as they scatter
Had you watch some children at play
Or wonder what was the matter?
As the day just slinked away

Did you ever stretch out a hand
Just because it was there
Have you wanted to give money away
Just to show that you care?

Did you take a ride in your car
Just to slip back—to a memory gone
Did you ever lay on your bed
Not answering the telephone?

Did you want to take a warm bubble bath
And soak in the tub—till you wrinkle?
Did you desire—an ice cream cone
Watching stars in the night sky—twinkle?

Do you meander along the seashore
Collecting sea shells in your path
Or peruse a "page turning" book
Hoping the story will last?

Did you gather a garden bouquet
Or take a walk when it pours

Play with your dog—till the end of the day
And having her begging for more

Ever stare at a refracting pool
And see your face as you gaze?
Did you ever—go back to school
Worrying if you'll make the grade?

Wandering down a street in your town
Whiffing some warm baking bread
Stopping along—and just window shop
It's the best day you've ever had.

Did you jump—into a cold pool
In the heat—of a mid summer's day?
Swim back and forth—for hours and hours
Just—so you can be cool?

Did you ever—sit in a chair
Formulating thoughts so deep
Have you ever—wanted to sing
Or desiring a good night's sleep.

Ever wanted to "just say No"
Instead of answering Yes
Just allowing God into your life
Because you know—He knows best!

Written by: Mara DeRose
August 27, 2008

Reflection

A new year is almost upon us
So we sit and talk, hand in hand
Thinking over the bad and good days
That God aloud us to span.

You go to work each morning
Quietly kissing me good bye
Checking on the children
Before you leave my side.

The kids wake up soon after
Breakfast is the next to go
Off to school for Robert
Sleep time for baby—OH

Next to make the beds
The telephone rings
It's my dear friend Judy
We talk of many things.

The quietness of these moments
Remembering back over the years
Talking in low voices
Knowing the end is near

We shall start the New year
With love we both can share
With our lovely children
And good friends that truly care.

As we pier into their faces
To see that all goes well
We look to the future
Sharing the past as well.

Sparklettes

Sparklettes caressing as it hit's the sand
As the waves come dancing by
And all around this peaceful beach
The gulls come flying high.

A rhythm all it's own
And kiss the specks of sand
And all about is stillness,
And a very Almighty man.

He walks besides the water
He's carrying a heavy load
It is my sin before me
He is my safe abode.

He is there my Father
Taking me by the hand
He has come to give me
And offer me another chance.

The gift is for my taking
I cannot sit and cry
For the day is almost over
And the promise, I can't deny.

Sparklettes on the water
Caressing of the shore
And not want for anything
For God's the one I adore.

Send an Angel

Send an angel for me Lord,
Send an angel for me
I am waiting on you Lord,
And my soul will be free
Everyday that I'm praying
Bring me home to your heart
Lift me up and I'll see Lord,
Take me home to your heart

I love you, don't you hear my plea
I'm on bended knee Lord,
I just need to be free…

Send an angel to me Lord,
Take my hand and we'll rise
I just need to be free Lord,
Take me into your skies.
Everyday as I'm praying
I am waiting to hear
That you are bringing me
Hope to stay with you dear.

I love you, don't you hear my plea
I'm on bended knee Lord,
I just need to be free.

Song Poem
Written by: Mara DeRose
March, 17, 2009

See My Pain

See my pain Lord, See my pain
See me standing out in the rain
How I am suffering, inside my brain
See my pain Lord, see my pain.

Hear my heart Lord, hear my heart
See my loving you while falling apart?
What do I do now, where do I go?
Hear my heart Lord, wherever I follow.

I am so lonely Lord, but know You are there
That's why I'm speaking in my despair
Im turning again Lord, I answer to YOU.
Don't look away Lord, because I love YOU.

See my pain Lord, Hear my own heart
I'm sad and lonely which path do I start?
You point the way Lord, give me a clue
I am here waiting and watching for you.

Seven Wonders

There are seven wonders in my world
And I consider each one each day.
I love and laugh and feel and hear
I see and hope and pray.
My Lord does guide my path I travel
He guides my wonders too
For without them in my daily life
I'd have nothing to offer you.

There are seven wonders in my world
And I try to live in peace
I love my neighbor as myself
I give when others cease
I feel when others suffer pain
And I hope for cures to come
I Pray and Pray the Rosary
For the wonders are for everyone.

There are seven wonders in my world
I offer them now to you
To go into your every day
And spread the Good Book too.
For one day soon you shortly hear
That He's now come for you.
So go and do all you can
By word, or deed in truth

For God's Mercy is ever flowing
As He watches over all
So take the seven wonders now
And you will never fall.
Remember to give your heart
your spirit your soul and mind
For God is watching from on high
His gifts are intertwined.

Shadow

Hello, my name is Shadow,
And I'm PURR-fect in every way
I maybe an old man now,
But I can still jump okay.

I am more black than white
As my fur is getting old
My eyes don't work as well
And I'm hardly ever cold.

I purr and purr when I am with Nannie
I love her cause you see
She gives me lots of lovies.
And her smile is there for me…

I love to visit Nannie
So I go downstairs to see
So I depend on Nannie
So I climb up on her knee.

My Papa brings me my food each night
And he washes out my dish
I can hardly wait to eat
I hope its tuna fish…

I wait at the door each night
For my Dad to have a rest
I know how tired he is,
So I won't jump up on his chest

I like it when my DAD and I
Get to sit and watch TV.

Then I know he's my special DAD
And I'm happy as can be…

I maybe old and my fur falls out
But I'm still able to see
That I'm so very lucky
That my Family loves me.

Sing Out, Sing Out

Sing out, sing out as you pray
Sing out, sing out everyday
Sing out, sing out with God's Praise
For today, is the day that God has made.

Sing out, sing out with His Praise
Sing out, sing out in every way
Sing out, sing out as you Pray
For today, God Proclaims, His only way.

Sing out, sing out with all your heart
Sing out, sing out and be apart
Sing out, sing out—from the very start
For today, is the way for a brand new start.

Sing out, sing out with your peace
Sing out sing out for sweet release
Sing out that your joy will never cease
For today is the day we'll live in peace.

Sing out, sing out as you pray
Sing out, sing out in every way
Sing out sing out with God's praise
For today, is the day love's come your way.

Written by: Mara DeRose
August 20, 2008

Inspired by God's love for me this morning. He put this little song on my lips in my praise to HIM…

Silhouette

Silhouette of my use to be
Reflections of the past and me
Rummaging around in my brain
Gathering strength to sustain
Borrowing pleasure as it comes
Silhouettes, one by one
Stretching forth across each page
Binding down, upon the stage
Composite of the girl within
Marveling at the place begin
Images buttered in my head
Unleashing moments while in bed
Silhouettes not in black and white
Fragments of compelling light
Moments when they come and go
In which direction, whose to know?
Seconds pass, and then take flight
Is this just an over-sight?
Now I lay me down to rest
I pray that I will do my best
Silhouettes when looked upon
Is this me, or have I gone?
Basic melody in me
I wonder who—Could it be?
Silhouettes on the shade at night
It hides the cover, in sweet delight.

Written by: Mara DeRose
September 7, 2008

Silver Freeze

In the rare beauty of a—silver freeze
Droplets cling to branches—on the trees
The silence of the snow floating—from on high
The sun's beams dance across—as if to sigh

The ground is covered in a—mantle of snow
The sparklettes glitter as the—sun's rays glow
Bouncing off the whiteness of—crystals there
As if it's caresses beauty—unaware

And in the distance I can—see a rose
The last of summer, as it's—holds it's pose
Jack Frost has touched it with a—gentile breeze
The magic of the icicles dangling—in the freeze.

From my window I can—feel the chill
As I see the children—upon the hill
With their sleds sliding—up then down
Laughter's infectious when they—hit the ground.

All is windswept and—all is still.
As I gaze at splendor upon—the rill
The silver frost has come but—it won't last
Soon the heat will melt each—blade of grass.

Oh, the beauty is a sight to see
Wish you were here to hold in memory
A calmness comes sweeping in my heart
Before long the iciness will begin to part.

Solitude

In the solitude of this morn
As I lay and try to sleep—
I hear the sounds of ocean waves
And my heart still wonders deep.

In the stillness of the dark
As it covers me for the night
And as I pray to my God
And hope for a heavenly light!

My heart is speaking to my Lord,
In solitude of deep respect
And I humbly ask of HIM
Forgive me all my debt.

The surf I hear is peaceful
As it dances at the shore
And through it all—His MERCY,
And a chance for ever more?

For this solitude comes at dawn
As I lay and try to pray
To ask My Jesus for his help
I ask HIM to please stay?

The moon shines on the water
Reflecting God's beauty at the beach
The dance that comes a creeping
Is slightly out of my reach.

The foam kisses the sand
As the creatures come to call

And all is peaceful on the shore
I hear the wind in call!

Oneness now with my God
The silent flicker cast
From a burning candle
My heart is home at last.

SOMEONE SPECIAL

(Dedicated to Kristen)

There's a special someone, that's as cute as she can be
She's always in my thoughts and in my mind
We're always together sharing lots of worldly things
she's so beautiful she's one of a kind.

Her little face just beaming, when she wakes up each morn
And she never forgets to share her love with me
You can tell by the way she smiles, she's as happy as can be
And I'll be there for her as long as she needs me.

This special little someone with eyes of sparkling blue
Sings her song each morning and I'm as proud as I can be
And this is how we share the love that's fresh and pure and true
No wonder I'll always sing this little special song to you!

Close your eyes and go to sleep,
Close your eyes and don't you peek
Sandman's coming soon my dear
Hush now little Baby!

Standing at the Altar

As we stand at the altar
Before our God and friends,
We will vow to one another
We will try to tackle every bend.

We will promise forever
That we have love enough today
To take us through each toil
And hardship along the way.

As our hearts and hands are melding
And we take this solemn vow,
We shall love one another
Without questioning when and how.

With the grace and beauty
And our dignity and poise
We will dance our way to happiness
Every blessing bringing joys.

As we turn to face each other
And the words ring in our ears
You are husband and wife now
Go in peace for all your years.

I will give to you my ring
Symbolizing my love for you
And in token you present to me
A heart reaching out to you.

Standing Up to Cancer

I'll stand up to Cancer,
I'll fight it with every ounce I can
I'll give my money for research
Until the answers are found.

I'll stand up to Cancer
I'll fight it with all of my might
I'll not be a part of the sufferings
When a cure could be in sight.

I'll stand up to Cancer
I'll do what I can each day
Research is truly the answer
So I'll give and I'll give as I pray.

Join me now and ask God
Find a cure for this deadly disease
Pray that He'll end all suffering
BEG HIM down on your knees.

Stay in the "Moment"

One must live their life in the Moment
Cause you can't live in the past.
You must journey each day as a lesson
And you must share what you can that will last.

You must Stay in the Moment everyday
Stop worrying for things that you don't own
You can adjust the way you are thinking
And you will enclose in your heart what you've sewn.

You must stay in the moment of each hour
And be true to yourself as best you can
If you give everyone the best of your self
Then the symphony of laughter is a hand.

So be advised that I'm giving you my best
And I'm offering this advise as I go
Stay in the Now and live the rest
And never put your issues on the show.

Do whatever you can do
Treat others as they would treat you
Be the best person you can be everyday
And I know God will be waiting there to guide you through...

Sudden Unplanned Changes

All of a sudden things happen in life
That I never realized possible before
Love, acceptance and happiness
Can it come in through my door?

Stepping stones and opportunities
Try and keep me on the right path
Satisfaction and fulfillment;
Obstacles become my abundant tasks.

Anxieties embrace my thoughts
And I can no longer function
And open my heart to enfolding moments
Safety is at this junction.

Sudden unplanned changes occur
Needing clarity for every worth
Diverse and ability to laugh at life
Is this here heaven on earth?

Powerful reminders speak to my soul
Response to my question in freeing delight
Amazingly my inner-self attentively listens
And I'm enriched by divine heights.

Every cleansing breath that I take
Rejuvenating my response too each chance
I nurture feelings by doing my best
Because I've got so much to sustain!

That's My Story

I wanted to share this day with you
And my heart went out to you
So, I called you on the phone,
I could tell, you were not alone,
So I hung up and I cried,
Knowing somehow that I tired
To keep from breaking down
Feeling like I was your clown
Now where do I go from here?
That's my story, and I'm sticking to it
Nothing left—but to go through it
Thought you really loved me,
Thought you cared,
Broken hearted—over things that we'd never share.

Next day met you on the street,
Thought that I was so indiscreet,
And I faced you and I said,
Wished I could have stayed in bed,
But again you lied to me
Telling me you'd soon be free
Wondering why I should believe
That you wanted her to leave
Now where do I go from here?
That's my story, and I'm sticking to it
Nothing left—but to go through it
Thought you'd give me
An answer true
Broken hearted—over YOU!

Sunset at Twilight

The sky wore it's jewelry of stars
On one mild and lovely night.
You whispered how you loved me
As we glanced up and held me so tight.

Colors were a memory
Buried for the night
But you saw a prism's painting
I envisioned black and white.

Waves squeezed the jetties
And filled the air with spray
The sea seemed so empty
The sun was slipping slowly away.

Yes, color was a memory
Buried by the night
But you saw a prism's painting
While I saw black and white.

Capture those elusive white caps
As they danced across your mind
And taken to the sunset at twilight
And our soul's are inter-twined.

TALK to the Lord

I talk to the Lord,
I speak to Him day and night
I pray to my God,
He carries me into His Light.

I ask Him each day
To help all His people along the way.
He guides me along
He gives me a song.

I don't know why HE is so generous to me
I hear his words and they do comfort me
I TRUST in HIS love and He takes me higher
Forgiveness I seek, and He offers His hand out to me
I need HIM inside, my heart and soul.

I talk to the Lord,
I pray each day for Peace
I welcome His assurance
For he's always besides me
I offer my life
And give him whatever He seeks
My heart opens wide, and gives me a feast.

I don't know why He's so Loving and wise
Is it that, I never open my eyes
To the life that is destine to be, my life for an eternity.

Thank You Father in Heaven

Thank you Father in heaven
For the help you've given me today
I wished there were better words
To express my love as I pray.

I thank you Father in heaven
For the gifts that you have shared
My heart is so very grateful…
I hope you can will hear

I thank you for helping me
When I ask for it in my prayers
You gave to me a flower
To be placed into my hair.

You are my redeemer,
And I always trust in You.
I thank you then my Father
In everything I say and do.

Just you and me dear Father
I am waiting now
And grant me another night,
That I may be a guiding light.

The Greatest Gift

I can't turn the clock back to days that use to be
I can't change the way you feel, what will be, will be
You've gone your way and I've gone mine, even though I can still see
I can't turn the clock back, to make you still love me.

When I heard your voice again, I could hardly speak
I wanted to tell you everything but inside I felt so weak
I still love and miss you, more and more each day
The greatest gift I ever got was loving you today.

If you could see inside my heart as well inside my head,
You'd know that love is everything…and believe what I have said
Yes, I still love and miss you, more and more each day
The greatest gift I ever got was loving you today.

Days have passed between us love
Since we kissed and said good-bye
Yet everyday I hoped and prayed, that you'd soon realize
Yes, I still love and miss you, more and more each day
The greatest gift I ever got was Loving YOU today!

Written by: Mara DeRose
May 17, 1974

The Man I Fell in Love With

He was all man with strong hands
And brown eyes that sometime cried
He was so tall that I felt small
And the kind of a man I fell in love with.

He was so smart right from the start
He gave his heart and he did his part
He was so tender that I surrendered
And the kind of man I fell in love with.

He was hopes and dreams and by all means
And the only one made me come undone
He was so good, and if we should
And the kind of man I fell in love with.

His thoughtful ways in all his days
And he held me tight each and every night
And he'd touch my hand, and we'd stand
Face to face, in our embrace.

Now this gentle man, with strong hands
And lips so sweet, made me complete
His gentle words, it just occurred
And the kind of man I fell in love with.

This Is My Last Chance

This is my last chance to make a difference in my life
This is my last chance to push away all strife
I have but once chance to do what my heart wants to vow
And free myself—to be myself—beginning now.

This is my last chance to transform my mind set today
I have but one more moderation so I can stay
Revolutionize my thinking, without a blink
And change myself, not blame myself…To think.

This is my last time to make a brand new start
And my last dance to show a brand new heart
I have but one more direction, to achieve my goal
And give myself, renew myself…or fold.

Melody of the Sea/The Wonder of the Sea

I want to go down to the seaside
And watch the ships sail away,
I've got to go down to the seaside
And watch the waves in the bay.

I love to hear the ocean's roar,
Feel the spray fly in my face,
Sea shells lying on it's floor
And the waves keeps up the pace.

I love to sit on a high perch,
And watch the birds fly by
I've got to sit on that high perch
And listen to their cry…

Listen can you hear it,
The Melody of the sea,
Racing, ranting raging
Just like she ought to be…

I love to walk on the sand dunes
And crack the seaweed's grass
Cavorting along the seashore
Until the sun's gone at last

Listen can you hear it,
The Melody of the sea,
Rolling, running, rising
Just like she ought to be…

I love to hear the ocean's roar,
See the spray fly in my face
Seashells lying on it's floor,
And the waves keep up the pace…

There Cannot BE

There cannot be a window, without a window pane
There can not be a door, without a sturdy frame
There cannot be a room without some walls around
There cannot be home without a family in town.

There cannot be a garden, without some grass and seeds
There cannot be a walkway without a path that leads
There cannot be a driveway, a place to walk and play
There cannot be a beauty without a Rose today.

There cannot be a village, without people around
There cannot be a highway, where travelers will be found.
There will not be a sun above, or moon or sea or stars
For God has given us birth as melodic as guitars.

I am so very lucky to have these and so much more
I have windows to open as well as every door
I have a room I call my own, to do with as I will
I am truly Blessed by God, and I pray there is no bill?

Written by: Mara DeRose
November 4th, 2008

There Is No Greater Blessing

There is no greater Blessing
than a friend who is there when things go awry
There is no greater Blessing
when a friend lends a hand without your asking
There is no greater Blessing
when your actions speak louder than any words could
There is no greater Blessing
Than a phone call is encouraging
There is no greater Blessing
When a friend gives you their heart
There is no greater Blessing
You feel their love surround you
There is no greater Blessing
That a friend who steps in
And finishes whatever needs doing
And never looks for reward, or ask in return.

Written by: Mara DeRose
February 8, 2009

Things

Arced rainbows and misty dewdrops
Starlight and flavorful lollipops
Moon beams and singing guitars
Yellow Buttercups and shooting stars
Roller blades and smiley faces
Ballet slippers and Angel traces
Autumn leaves and winter snows
Twittering birds and gusty winds blow
Colorful parcels and children at play
I wonder IF it's a Holiday?
Dogs barking and kitten's purr
Balloons floating, and winter's burr
Abundant grasses and voters dilemma
Sticky buns and rawhide leatha

This Is a Foundation

This is a foundation of my new world with you
I feel you around me and I know it's true
You lift me higher with just the touch of your heart
I know for certain that it's just the start.

This is the beginning of a life all so new
I've sung my heart out and I given it to you
I've trusted every minute, since my heart felt your touch
Knowing forever that I love you so much...

This is the launching of a life transformed
Listen to my heart beat and be informed
When our eyes met and my feet stood still
I knew forever you are mine, you are mine, you are mine...
Cause you always will.

Lift me higher, take me away, carry me off to a distant place
Tell me you love me, whisper to me, that I inspire you...and what will be will be.
Life me higher, take me away, carry me off to a distant place
Tell me you love me, whisper to me, you'll always be there, just for me.

This is the beginning of a life with you
I sense you around me, and you know it's true
You send me floating till I can't go any higher
I know you love me, as you always inspire.

So lift me higher, take me away, carry me off to a distant place.
Tell me you love me, whisper to me, I'll always be in your life, eternally...
Lift me higher, take me away, carry me off to a distance place
Tell me you love me, whisper to me, You'll always be here, just for me.

Time

Time to hold you nice and tight
Time to kiss you, morning noon and night
Time to squeeze you and take your hand
Time to make you understand
Time to give you all that I can
Time to show you that I'm your loving woman

Time to walk you to your door
Time to whisper forever more
Time to take the next step in life
Time to make you my man for life
Time to please you make dreams come true
Time to say the words "I do!"

Time to say good nighty night
Time to dance into the light
Time to move so nice and slow
Knowing which way we should go
When I turn off all the lights
Time again to hold you tight.

Time I give my heart to you
All that your body needs me to do
When we kiss and hold on to
I just pray we'll make it through
Time to give you all I can
Time to show you that I'm your loving woman…

Written by: Mara DeRose
January 14, 2009

Treasures of My Heart

When I wake up each morning
I thank my God above
For all the gifts you've given me
And share with me YOUR love.

I have two eyes, two hands and feet
I have two ears to hear
My heart keeps beating rhythmically,
From year, to year, to year!

The treasures of my heart
Are the gifts I cannot share
I didn't think it was possible
To dream, a dream so rare.

The many songs and poems written
By me with your divine help
I thank you now my Father in Heaven
Is my true treasures and my wealth…

Try As I May

Try as I may, to forget the time of day
Try as I may, the thought won't go away
Your warmth, your smile, your kiss well worth while
The magic of your touch, I love you so much.

You say that you love me, now do you love me true?
You say that you need me and you will see me through

You promised forever, that love would always be
Now all that is left now, is for me to set your free…

Two Different Places

Two different places, two different spaces
Tow different worlds apart
Two different people holding each other
It's beginning to break my heart

We came from two different places
Yet we knew from the start
We were two different lovers, two different covers
Now we're just drifting apart.

Yes, two different places, two different spaces,
Two different lovers but then
Two different strangers hurting each other
Now we can only be friends.

Part of me is with you now
Part of me was with you then
Part of me is questioning still
Part of me is hurting now

Part of me is searching while
Has our love really come to an end?

Two Thousand and Eight

At 4.49…waiting on line—to buy gasoline
How can I plan—or have the car stand—until the lights green?
And At 4.19—a gallon of milk,—I can't feed my kids
The prices these days,—just blows me away,—cause I can't get a raise.
The prices so high,—I can't even buy,—a cup of coffee today
I can't plan a trip, or go by ship…I've no money to pay.
In two-thousand and eight—the cost is so great, I've lost my job
And what do I eat, with no money for meat, I eat corn on the cob…
My mortgage is high, we're just getting by, no money to spare
I go to my bank, with an empty tank, and my banker says "No!"
I shop at the store, looking for more, bargains for food
I clip my coupons, and cash all my bonds, while just holding on.
Taxes are more than ever before, but got a rebate
It's not much I know, but it helps the flow—watching my money go!
It's back to school time, it costs more than a dime, to purchase supplies
I hear from my kids, mommy please won't you give, money for treats
I feel like a heal, cause I can't conceal, I've no money to give…
What can I do, with no money for shoes, so I walk where I live
I hope today, a job comes my way, and I am employed.
When the days done, I turn to the one, my faith is restored.
This great USA is great, so they say, but I am in need
I'll send SOS, for money—less stress, cause I'm in a mess.
Don't ask me how, we'll manage somehow, to get through distress
For we're holding on, facing each dawn, we're just moving along.

Written By: Mara DeRose
July 29, 2008

Un-Day

It's not your anniversary
It's not your birthday either
Nor is it April Fool's day
Nor Easter time however
It's not Funny Valentine's
Nor is it 4th of July
It's just an UN-day for you—from me
That's why I'm standing by.

St Patty's Day, or Memorial Day
Are great holidays I admit
Veteran's day, nor Halloween
Or turkey Day—you bet.
President's day has come and gone
There's always Columbus day too
But the only UN- day I care about
It the time I spend with you…

Christmas and New Year's EVE
They—have come and gone
But my dreams for you will linger
In my heart's own sweet song
It doesn't have to be a holiday
To let you know I'm near
For it's the everyday UN-DAY
Just to show you that I'm here.

Written by: Mara DeRose
February 12, 2009

Up in Nova Scotia

Up in Nova Scotia, surrounded by the sea,
Lies a city known as Halifax, that's where I long to be—

There are lots of friendly faces,
no mater where you go
The people there are happy
and their pace is fairly slow—

In the middle of this city,
is a citadel on high
The tourists come to visit
with relics of years gone by—

The old town clock still sits there,
the cannons fire a round
It happens everyday at noon,
and the sea air is abound—

There are ships from all around the world
in the harbor for all to see
There's a garden and an old bandstand,
these memories flash back to me

Halifax is old but quaint,
but has so much to offer
It's many shops it's scenic shores,
I don't know why I left her—

Travel here by car bus or plane,
or ships that sail or railroad train
No matter which way you decide,
you'll be so happy you've taken the ride

Yes, I'm a Nova Scotian,
and this I'm proud to say
I'll be coming back again,
every chance that comes my way…

Unscripted

Each day God grants me an unscripted day
Upon which I must live
Along the way I edit and pray
I've given all I can give!

Unscripted, and peaceful
Merciful and kind
Grateful and thankful
To all of mankind.

Each day I wake up
And find without doubt
That God's love is showing
The message is out

I search for the answers
For questions I've got
I need to know
What's life all about?

Unscripted and undefiled
It's up to me, to do my rhyme
I love the Lord with all of my heart
I thank him with a joy that's sublime

Unscripted and blank
I do what I want
My soul is longing
For PEACE to flaunt.

So in my prayer,
I humbly ask
For PEACE for our world
And help with my task

Vacation

Been there, done that,
Bought the tee shirt,
Mailed the post cards
Wore the hat,
Saw the sights,
Spent all the money,
Visited with family,
Turned to plastic
Ate a Burrito,
Saw the cactus
And the Palm trees,
Took the boat trip,
Got a sun burn,
Shot the pictures,
Watched the squirrel
Talked to the tourists,
Got directions,
Won some card games
Laughed till my tummy ached,
Rode the copter,
Experienced Grand Canyon,
Sang the songs,
Picked an orange,
Played with the cat,
Drank all the water,
Ate oatmeal with brown sugar,
Packed my bags
Flew six hours to home,
Told the stories,
Printed the pictures,
Wished I could do it...
All over again.

Wait a Minute

Wait a minute—won't you please
For I'm down on my knees
For I love you—and I beg you to stay

Wait a minute—can't you see
You're the only one for me
I will love you—until my dying day.

Wait a minute,—take your time
Before you make up your mind
My heart is yours,—please don't throw it away.

Wait a minute—one more time
Before I drink too much wine
I can't take it—Please don't break it today

Wait a minute…Before you go
I just had to let you know
I'll be waiting,—for your answer—will it say

Wait a minute—won't you please
Cause I'm here on my knees
For I love you…And want you—I pray

Country Song Poem
Written by: Mara DeRose
Nov. 15, 2008

Wash Me Oh Lord

Wash me from my sins Oh Lord?
Wash away all Pride?
Wash away all stains Oh Lord,
I've no place to hide.
Wash away all angry thoughts?
Wash my anger too
Wipe off every hurtful thing
Let a better soul shine through?

Wash away all hurt Oh Lord?
Take away all pain
Wash me clean and pure Oh Lord,
Standing in the rain.
Wash away any lust and greed,
Open up my heart
Allow a prayerful creed
Be a brand new start?

Wash away all wants and needs
Forgive my possessive mind
Wash away all crimes I've done
Enrobe me with your sign?
Wash away my body Lord?
Wash away all pain
Wash away all sins Oh Lord,
My soul is heavily stained.

Wash away all earthly wants
Guide me along the right road?
I truly Love YOU LORD
Forgive me for everything I've sewed?

As you wash away my body,
Wash away my mind
Take me to a better place
I want to help mankind?

Wash My Body Clean

Wash my body clean?
And turn me towards the light.
Wash my body clean
Preparing me for the night?
Wash my body clean,
And point me towards the road
I will follow YOU,
Unburden the heavy load.

Wash my body clean
And cleanse my soul today?
Wash my body clean
Please listen while I pray?
Wash my body clean
And show me what I must do
To share in Your body and blood
And worship my whole life through?

Wash my body clean
Taking away all pain,
Wash my body clean
My soul shouldn't have a stain
Wash away my struggles
Turn them inside out
I will follow YOU,
My soul will gratefully shout.

We Share a Secret of Life

Within each of us for moments before
The passion of a few fleeting moments
It's the Peak" that opens the door.

Our eye lids now—so heavy
AS the close of a long, busy day
He whispers to me, "I love you!"
Farewell to another day.

As sleep now creeps over our minds
Our bodies lying side by side
Sharing the closeness of the moment
Our dream begins to unwind.

We Stand United

We stand united in America, we pledge to make a change
We stand excited in America our history we try and re-arrange
We stand invited in America we'll do all that we can do
We stand delighted in America, until our work is shinning through.

We can join our neighbor we can lend a hand
We can offer whatever it takes to mend the land
We can give of ourselves and make a new plan
We can share whatever we make, as united we stand.

So begin today, do whatever you can do
Try your very best you can see it through,
For America needs help—it's your country too
Just reach out and unite, in everything you do.

Written by: Mara DeRose
January 19, 2009

Inspired by the Inauguration of Barack Obama

Wedding Anniversary Song for My Parents

50th anniversary

Today, is the first day, for the rest of our lives
You're standing besides me, won't you stay by my side?
Our love has never been so deep or so true,
That's why today, my heart is speaking to you—

Together forever, we've seen our love grow
Sharing and caring together we'll show
Like flowers that blossom and come into bloom
That's why my heart speaks "I love only YOU."

Days come and Days go, and love never ends
Like the ring on your finger, I put way back then,
Our love has survived the true test of time.

It doesn't seem possible fifty years have gone by.
Fifty years of our loving, how quickly they fly
Like birds have taken to the blue sky above
How happy you've made me with the gift of your love.

Now as I stare at the love on your face,
I still feel the warmth of your tender embrace—
Just the touch of your hand, or the glance of your eye
Brings all these emotions, and a tear to my eyes!

Yes, today is the first day for the rest of our lives
And everyday a first day, fill with our cries
If I only knew now, what I should have known then
I'd ask you to marry me all over again…???

Now as I stare at the love on your face
I still feel the warmth of your tender embrace

Year have waked away many a tear
Now love has erased them with each passing year.

Written by: Mara DeRose
Dec 4, 1991

Honor of my parents 50th wedding anniversary!

When All Is Said and Done

When all is said and done, oh Lord
I thank you on my knees
For every gift you've given
And for everything you please.

When all is said and done, Oh Lord,
My heat is saying Thanks
I offer you my sufferings
Along with aches and pains.

When all is said and done, Oh Lord,
I beg of You this today,
If you can grant me help
And more beauty to my day.

When all is said and done, Oh Lord,
I hope you'll ask me in
For I am giving you my life
And wish to enter in?

When all is said and done, Oh Lord,
And leave this world behind
Let me not disgrace you
Or that of all human kind…

When all is said and done, Oh Lord,
And I am through on earth,
That I may continue to worship You
And grant us a rebirth.

When all is said and done, Oh Lord,
Allow the sunshine begin

Show me the way I can please you
And forgiveness for all my sin?

When all is said and done, Oh Lord,
I offer to you this day
My heart my soul, my hands
This I do humbly pray…

When I Can't Sleep

When I can't sleep at night,
I turn to HIM in prayer
I often listen to the sounds
The ocean and it's fair

I pay attention to the waves
As they come dancing in
And I can hear the oceans roar
In solitude begin

When I can't sleep at night
I sometimes lay so still
I sense as if my heart should rest
And the echoes over the hill.

The music swells over the waves
And again my thoughts are here
If only I could settle down
And find a cheery pier.

The vision of the seaweed
As it lays on ocean's floor
And the ebbing of the tides
Fills my mind to explore.

When I Get Up Each Morning

When I get up each morning
And saunter through the day;
I offer psychological nourishment
To those I meet along the way.
I pray to God My Father
And to Mother Mary to approve
My words and deeds
And I ask for holy blessings
So they will intercede.

When I get up each morning
And face the day ahead
I remember in my heart
What our Lord and Master said.
To love one another as
You would wanted to be loved
And always ask for guidance
From my heart to the LORD above

Written by: Mara DeRose
June 15, 2007

Where Is This DREAM Called Happiness?

Why can't I find some happiness?
I keep on searching and find loneliness
Time is fleeting, and I want, I guess
Where is this dream called Happiness?

Why can't I find someone to love?
I keep on grasping and ask heaven above
My dreams evade me, so I need a shove
Where is this dream called Happiness?

Someday, some way, I hope to find
A kindred spirit, that will make me shine
I want to satisfy my hungry mind
Where is this dream called happiness?

I let go of trying to force his love
I've asked for answers from above
Empower me so I can find true love
Where is this dream called happiness?

Remaining silent is so hard to do
Emerging feelings have me wanting you,
I search for answers but have no clue
Where is this dream called Happiness?

My life has shadows and uncertainties
And I am not promised any guarantees,
Quench my thirst or let me be
Where is this dream called Happiness?

Whisper What I Should Do

Whisper, what I should do Oh Lord,
For I am lacking for guidance
Whisper and tell me what road to chose
For I am lost and need a new advance

Whisper what I should do My God
If You can point out the way
For I am nothing without You Lord
I trust You everyday.

Whisper to my heart and mind,
Give me the best direction
For I will follow You for all time
You have the answers for my reflection.

Grant the world Peace on earth
Cure all the diseases
Bring about a heavenly mirth
And bring about all that pleases.

Hear my prayer in whisper Oh Lord,
For I will try each day and night
I ask your blessed Mother Mary
To guide me through to the light.

Whisper What I could do My God,
May I never be parted from You
I am listening with all my heart
Because of my great reverence too!

Who Will

Who will dry your tears today
Who will wash them all away
Who will help you while you sleep
Who will guide you—slumber deep
Who will believe in you so strong
Who will teach you right from wrong
Who will over look all fears
And will guide you through the years
Who will sing sweet lullabies
Who will hold you when you cry
Who will offer prayers for you
Who will chase away the blue
Who will take you by the hand
Guide you while you search the land
Who will cry when you are low
And will wait when you are slow
Who will be there day and night
Even help you fly your kite
Who will carry when you can't walk
Who will be there to teach you talk
Who is there that you know
Who will love you, do you know?

I am that person, I am you see
I am Mother, holding thee
I am your guiding steps you take
I am the one who will bake
I will chase away each tear
I will be the one to cheer
I will always stand by you
I will help you find your shoe
I will try and be the one

Who will love you, only Son…
I have taught you to read and write
I have watched you day and night
I have listened to your pleas

I'm the one upon my knees
Giving thanks to my God above
I have given you so much love.
I will dry away each tear
I am with you…year to year.
You now speak with dignity
You do walk with impunity
You're a man now on the go
I seek no credit, for I love you so.

Written by: Mara DeRose
July 28, 2008

WHY

Why am I living?
Why am I here
I don't have the answers
The futures un-clear
Why do I wander
Why can't I see
That young woman
I so long to be.

Why am I unhappy
Why do I cry
Everyday, every minute
I know I will die
Why do I want "things"
That never mean much
Is it that I'm greedy
Or searching for touch?

WHY can't I un-do
The things that I've done
I need to clear up
Things with your Son.
Why should I hold on
TO memories in my pas
One day I know
I'll be resting under green grass.

Why don't I leave life,
In God's helpful hands
I don't have the answers
Questions older than sand.
He knows my weakness
He knows my flaws
He knows my heart aches
I don't know the cause.

Wonder of Wonders

Wonder of wonders—can this be real?
I've finally fallen in love
With a man that is so very special
He means the world to me.

When I awake each morning,
And I feel my heart begin to pound
I talk to myself and say, "Is this the day?"
I'll finally be with this special man
And it's wonderful, happy rainbow kind of day.

Even thou' I've never ever heard you say my name
I have a lot of sensuous dreams
I feel your arms about me as you gently touch my hand
When I know you have never touched me—but only in my dreams.

Wonder of wonders can this be so?
I've passionately, fallen in love
Is it all a dream and my imagination?
How do I know it's true?
I'll have to wait and trust what will be will be.

Words On Play

Emotional embellishment
Psychological nourishment
Religious Fulfillment
Therapeutic resistance
Occupational necessities
Spiritual awareness
Physical agility
Numerical indifference
Logistical compliancy
Invasive performance
Gratuitous indulgence
Primitive inter-structure
Poignant suggestions
Nautical subversive
Compliance reactions
Judicial reliance
Vocal assurance
Visual impediment
Monetarily adjustment
Atonement willingness
Figuratively speaking
Harlequin patterns
Emphatic questions
Robotic actions
Egregious crimes
Indigenous species
Platitudes of mercy
Fruitful irony

Written by: Mara DeRose
June 18, 2008

Yesterday, Today and Forever

I have loved you Lord,
Yesterday, today and forever
And I thank you Lord,
For each of my endeavors
My heart offers to you
All the treasures of this world
And I turn to you
With my heart unfurled
Yesterday, today and forever.

Give me patience dear Lord,
With my daily tasks
I need your graces Lord,
This is what I'm humbly ask
For yesterday is gone
And today is really here,
And if tomorrow never comes
I will try and persevere

Life is short, dear Lord,
And my soul belongs to you
I give them freely dear Lord,
I offer now to you
Take my yesterdays Lord,
And today will see me through
For tomorrow Lord,
I hope to be with you.

You Sent Me A Blessing Today

Oh Dear God, I thank you from my heart
You gave me such a special friend,
She brought to me a little gift to remind me…
How fortunate I've truly been.

I had lost my Holy Medals
After a difficult surgery
I hope that now they are blessing someone else
And that they will have a discovery.

Of St Jude, Mother Mary and St PadrePio,
My heart is truly over-joyed
But of course, I know you know,
The kingdom is our reward.

The Blessing You have given this day
Has filled me up to the brim
I don't know what I could ever do
Without such a wonderful friend.

How Blessed are we to have the Saints
To protect and pray for us each day.
But in order to get this Blessing we
Must get down on our knees and pray.

Dedicated to Mel Alessi
Who replaced my holy medals that I lost during my recovery from Brain Surgery on August 29, 2005

You Are My Valentine, My Love

You are my Valentine, my love
You make my heart shine, my love
You give me strength when I'm weak
You lift me high, when you speak
You help me give when I've nothing left
You bring me love, all I can get
You are My Valentine, my love
I'm glad you're in my heart and soul.

You are my Valentine my friend
You teach me how I can always lend
You make my heart beat rapidly
You take me where I want to be
You taught me new and special things
You gave to me my wedding ring
You taught my heart how it should sing
You are my love, my everything.

You are my Valentine, my love
You were sent down from heaven above
You share with me a life of wedded bliss
You always share with me a kiss
You are within my heart to stay
Our love will never ever fade away
You are my special Valentine
I hope you'll be forever mine…

You Filled My Soul

You have opened my ears Oh Lord,
You have opened my eyes.
You have lifted me high O Lord,
To reach the sky.
You have touched my mind Oh Lord,
You have guided me too—
All the tasks you have given Lord,
You have carried me through.

You have filled my soul Oh Lord,
You have shown through the night
You have filled my heart Oh Lord,
To reach the high heights
You have taught me how to live,
And what I must do.
To gain eternal life
My whole life through.

Exalted—Adored—My sweet Lord,
You filled my prayer
You opened me up Oh Lord,
So I wouldn't despair.
I'll continue to pray Oh Lord,
With hopeful delight
I offer this prayer to You
Each day and each night.

You have filled my soul Oh Lord
You have sheltered my dream
You have given me everything
That I'll ever need
You have offered me life, Oh Lord
By bringing to me
The gift of your suffering
You set our souls free.

Chorus:

1) You filled my dreams. You answered them too, you filled my spirit, deep inside, my whole life through

2) You filled my heart, You filled my soul, you filled my heart, my mind, my soul, making me whole

Written by: Mara DeRose

You Have Not

You have not abandoned me Lord,
It is I who has forsaken you
You are here when troubles soars
And you have seen me through

I have sinned against your rules
And I deserve to pay!
I will try with all my heart
To abstain them right away.

Forgive me Lord for what I've done
And what I've failed to do
For I'm weak and sinful Lord
But this I'm begging YOU?

Wash away my sins My God
Wash me through and through
For I desire to be free again
To live my whole life through.

You have not deserted me Lord
It is I who had vacated you
I hope you've heard my voice in prayer
Because I love you through and through.

Written: April 10, 2009
Good Friday

You Mean Everything to Me

Strong rhythms of words are flowing forth to dissipate the night
As if to announce "You are not alone," and uplifting us to the light
Celebration of my genuine love, I offer now to you
Take it as a sign of trust, I extend and share with YOU!

Because we have shared a vision of promise, and what the future might hold,
I feel a sense of accomplishment, and if I'm not too bold
My gift of life to the both of you, is as sustaining as can be
That's why I say today, in a nurturing way, "You mean everything to me!"

I have invested in you my guidance, and tender loving care
Please handle this love I offer to you, because nothing can compare
Unity of our hearts, and blood confronts me in difficult times, Aspiring
desires of a Mother's Love, harmony and rhyme!

Prevailing responsibilities have taken me to a different point of view
Sweet prayer sweeps over my soul, and I haven't got a clue,
Life-affirming choices, made within your hearts, accompanies as you go,
Know that this Mother is ministering her trust, and allowing her love to flow.

So put your worries aside, and trust in God, in all circumstances
Trust in each other and share your journey through time, and your finances
Dedicate your efforts, invest in yourself and you will hold the key
That is why I've come this day cause, "You mean EVERYTHING to ME!

Written by: Mara DeRose
October 20, 1999

Dedicated to my children
Robert Jr and Kristen

You Never Cease to Amaze me Lord

You never cease to Amaze me Lord,
It's snowing on the first day of spring
The crocus' and daffodils are peaking up
To see what You will bring

You never cease to amaze me Lord,
The birds are building their nests
They are gathering twigs and strings
And they only stop to take a little rest.

You never cease to amaze me Lord
The trees are all beginning to bud
It won't be very long, my Lord,
In the air there are signs of true love.

You never cease to amaze me Lord,
The grass is turning brighter green through the snow
The winds are blowing more softly now
While the children playing while they are on the go.

You never cease to amaze me Lord,
You give me more than I could ever want or need
I never have to ask for anything
You fill my heart with gladness as I read.

You never cease to amaze me Lord,
I thank you daily for all you've done
I'll continue to pray each day
For I know You are my truth...Holy ONE.

Written by: Mara DeRose
March 20, 2009

Your Birthday Dear Mother

Your birthday dear Mother is tomorrow
I'm still sad, I need to borrow
Your courage, your kindness, your love for the family
Your caring and sharing, and always applying
Your ten year in heaven—can it be that long
I'm lonely and miserable since you've been gone.

Your birthday dear Mother comes tomorrow
What can I do, to erase all my sorrow?
I hear you laughter still in my ears
I relive those moments every day a new tear
Oh Mother how I miss you, I wished you were here
My heart is still aching as I pass through each year.

Your birthday dear Mother is tomorrow
I'd still need your guidance, in all of my sorrow
You stay with me, worry with me, and in my prayer
Your sweet smiles comes to me, the gray in your hair.
I love you dear Mother, I miss you too
Happy Birthday in Heaven, Happy birthday to you.

Written by: Mara DeRose
Nov 4th, 2008

You're All I've Ever Wanted

You're all I've ever wanted for Christmas
I've searched and searched my whole life through
I've dreamed that one day soon,
I'd find you, and hold you—I do

You're all I've ever wanted for Christmas
And so far I've had quite a few
Each one is special and memorable
But that's because I now have found you…

You're all I've ever wanted for Christmas
My husband, my sweetheart, my friend
You've give me two children
And you've shared with me many a bend.

You're all I've ever wanted for Christmas
When those church bells chime to come
I'll sit beside you and hold your hand
We'll share another Christmas Eve again.

Show Me the Way

I've Come to the End

I've come to the end my friend
I've walked a straight line
I've given it all I had
And life's been sublime

I've come to the close of night
And dawn springs anew
I am refreshed in the light
I'm questioning who

I've put away foolish things
I've made a new life
I rest in a gathering place
My heart sees the light.

And when my days end my friend
And God whisks me away
I hope you'll remember me
On a day like today.

So words have been on my mind
Both day into night
I hope that they've entertained
Now have a great flight.

So without a sad farewell
I'll miss you my friend
We've come down a long hard road
For this is the end...